# CHANGING THE MILITARY CULTURE OF SILENCE

SAMUEL M. RHODES

authorHOUSE®

*AuthorHouse™*
*1663 Liberty Drive*
*Bloomington, IN 47403*
*www.authorhouse.com*
*Phone: 1-800-839-8640*

*First published by AuthorHouse 2/24/2010*

*ISBN: 978-1-4490-4275-2 (e)*
*ISBN: 978-1-4490-4273-8 (sc)*
*ISBN: 978-1-4490-4274-5 (hc)*

*Library of Congress Control Number: 2009914344*

*Printed in the United States of America*
*Bloomington, Indiana*

*This book is printed on acid-free paper.*

## Samuel M. Rhodes
Command Sergeant Major Retired
Battle with PTSD and Suicide

# "Changing the Military Culture of Silence"

Mr. Sam Rhodes' warm personality captivates audiences as he speaks on coping with Suicide and Post Traumatic Stress Disorder. He inspires others by teaching how to build Psychological Resilience.

He has been invited to speak on regular occasions to Active, Guard, and Reserve Component units around the country including: Soldier Support Institute, Fort Jackson; School of Command Preparation, Fort Leavenworth; Fort Benning NCO Academy; Fort Gordon; Fort Polk; Fort Bliss; Fort Leonard Wood; Fort Campbell; Fort Irwin and 2d Stryker Cavalry Regiment Germany; the Massachusetts, Rhode Island, and Kentucky National Guards. He also has traveled to the Boston Veterans Administration Hospital and spoke to numerous groups of homeless veterans. In addition, he has held speaking engagements at many more events, including the Department of Defense Suicide Prevention Conference at the Hyatt Regency in San Antonio, Texas in January 2009 and to many other organizations.

Mr. Sam Rhodes has voluntarily worked with numerous organizations focused on "Changing the Military Culture of Silence" when dealing with mental health issues. His unique background includes over 29 years service in the Army, where he held numerous enlisted leadership positions culminating in his assignment as a Brigade Command Sergeant Major. He has served in Operation Iraqi Freedom I, II, and III, with a total of 30 months of combat experience accumulated from April of 2003 to November of 2005.

Mr. Sam Rhodes' unique approaches, style and personal courage have been featured on NBC 38 "Unity with Pam", in the Fort Benning Bayonet, Fort Gordon Signal, and Fort Jackson Leader newspapers and the Benning TV. He has received accolades from the Chief of Staff of the Army, General George W. Casey; Sergeant Major of the Army, Kenneth O. Preston; the Defense Center of Excellence for Mental Health General Laurie Sutton; LTG Whitcomb; and Rosemarie Annese, Vice President & Blue to Gold Liaison, Blue Star Mothers, MA Chapter 1. Additionally, Lockheed Martin has honored Mr. Sam Rhodes and the phenomenal contributions he has made to the community with their 2009 Community Service and Global Excellence Award for Building Effective Relationships.

Mr. Sam Rhodes is a graduate of TUI University with both a Bachelors and Masters Degree in Business Administration and is actively involved in the House for Heroes and the Wounded Warrior Horsemanship and Post Traumatic Stress Outreach Programs, which he initiated at Fort Benning.

Mr. Sam Rhodes has seen the after-effects of losing two great company commanders and watching as their bodies were placed in bags. His personal keynote speeches are packed with practical content, and extraordinary personal stories. Your audience will be informed, inspired and motivated to take immediate positive actions.

## Keynote Topic Psychological Resilience:

- Make Connections
- Avoid Seeing Crisis as Insurmountable Problems
- Accept That Change Is a Part of Living
- Move Toward Your Goals
- Take Decisive Actions
- Look for Opportunities for Self-Discovery
- Nurture a Positive View of Yourself
- Keep Things in Perspective
- Maintain a Hopeful Outlook
- Take Care of Yourself

**Key Learning Points:**

- ► Fixing the Problem only begins the process of personal recovery
- ► Shift from Blame and Shame to Taking Personal Responsibility
- ► A Hard Hitting Wake-Up Call
- ► Continuing Education has helped Significantly

**Credentials:**

- ► Author: "Changing the Culture of Silence," March 2010
- ► Author: Post Traumatic Stress Disorder Impacts all Levels of Leadership
- ► Professional Forum Infantry Magazine July-August 2007
- ► Author: "Battle of a Lifetime," Lockheed Martin Employee Perspective Column November 2008
- ► Author and contributor: US Army PTSD video released by AMEDD January 2009
- ► Wounded Warrior Horsemanship Program with WTB, Fort Benning, GA

---

**National Center for Post Traumatic Stress Disorder**
**(800) 296-6300**
**www.ncptsd.va.gov**
**Military One Source**
**(800) 342-9647**
**(If overseas precede number with U.S. access code)**

# CONTENTS

# INTRODUCTION

After twenty-nine years of military service, I retired in January 2009. I spent three tours in Iraq and it has begun a new chapter in my service to his country and comrades. In dealing with my own struggle with Post Traumatic Stress Disorder (PTSD), I have become an inspiration for members of the military nationwide, sharing experience with Veteran's and Active Duty Members and I encourage them to address and seek help for psychological health issues. As a advocacy about the importance of seeking help among members of the military is not only saving lives, but also helping to overcome the stigma associated with mental health issues. I was awarded the Combat Infantry Badge, Bronze Star 1st Oak Leaf, Legion of Merit, seven Meritorious Service Medals, and numerous other awards. I have attended every NCOES from PLDC to Sergeant Major Academy. I hold a Master's Degree in Business Administration and currently work as a project manager for Lockheed Martin, which is committed to my vision of helping my fellow warriors by gracefully allowing me to take these opportunities to share his story. I am also a devoted husband and father; I am married to Cathy Rhodes, formerly of Lebanon, Ohio. We have six children and seven grandchildren. CSM

Rhodes's free time is spent working with organizations across the country to "Change the Culture of Silence."

# CHAPTER 1

## Biography of Samuel M. Rhodes, Sr.

On January 29, 1961, I was born in Ringgold, Georgia, to Martha McClure Rhodes and Willie Burl Rhodes, as life would have it. Let's begin by talking about my hero father, Willie B. Rhodes, and his twin brother Earl Rhodes, born on Independence Day, July 4, 1920. They decided to join the war at a young age. Burl and Earl left to go to war by way of Camp Stewart. Burl decided to become a medic in the Army, not knowing what the future held, just wanting to defend his country and do his part. As it turns out, he may have done just that without a lot of effort.

During the Battle of New Guinea, Rhodes was put to the test. A fellow Soldier, his Commander, Marvin Griffin, was seriously injured. Without hesitation, Rhodes made a decision that would impact his life forever. Griffin was bleeding from his wounds; Burl's natural instinct of caring kicked in; he maneuver through fire, though seriously injured himself, to Griffin's side. He stabilized him enough to prepare him to move back toward a safe area for evacuation. Rhodes carried Marvin Griffin to safety, and he fully recovered. Rhodes did not know the impact of what he had done; he received numerous Presidential Citations for bravery and was awarded the Silver Star for his actions that day as well as many other military medals. Burl liked to talk about democracy and the home of the brave, but he rarely spoke of his own unique courage in World War II and his individual suffering from nightmares and symptoms of PTSD in the late seventies until his death on May 19, 1984.

Marvin Griffin later became Georgia's Lieutenant Governor and was seen as the successor to Governor Herman Tallmadge; Griffin won the governorship in 1954. Governor Marvin Griffin would not forget his friend. When the Governor was sworn in, Willie B. Rhodes was standing on the podium beside him. In 1955 and each following year, Marvin Griffin travelled to Burl's hometown to ride in the Independence Day parade with Burl Rhodes. A self-educated man, much like his fellow hero Alvin York, the Medal of Honor winner from Jamestown, Tennessee, Burl was proud to have served his country in its time of need. Like his son, he still had nightmares about his fiercest battles in war, but it didn't deter his love for his country and his fellow man. Willie B. Rhodes was flag-waving American for sure.

At the age of six years old, I started receiving contact with Mr. Marvin Griffin's wife. "How are you doing?" she asked. "I am Mrs. Griffin, Marvin's wife. He wants me to see how you're doing and send you something. What do you need?"

I remember those words like it was yesterday. I was born to a poor family, and my mom and dad separated when I was five years old, in 1966, so I found myself amazed by her words. I didn't know what to say; I remember asking my mom to talk. The next thing I remember, about two weeks later, I received a package of clothes. I was surprised; it wasn't my birthday or Christmas. My other brother and sisters looked at me and asked, "Why is Marvin getting something?" Yes, my father named me after the Governor, so I had big shoes to fill from the start. I would receive calls, letters, and packages, mostly from Mrs. Griffin, for the next decade until she passed away in 1978. The entire time I was growing up, I was mentored by Mr. Griffin as well as both of his wives. They encouraged me toward being a successful individual in life. My values were born of great mentorship from the Governor and his wife and my own parents. Governor Griffin offered to pay for my college; however, he developed cancer soon after his first wife's death in 1978. He later died in 1982 after a long battle with cancer.

Truly a different life for a poor country boy from north Georgia. I grew up knowing what was right and wrong. I also realized that a lot of kids around us had more than we could dream of. My mom decided not to get divorced from my father for thirteen years. Right before I graduated from high school in 1979, she got divorced from him. Prior to graduation, I only made one call to Mr. Griffin. I wasn't a genius in high school, so science and English always got the best of me. As I inched closer to getting out of school, it became tougher. At the age of sixteen, I moved out of my home and into a studio apartment in Fort Oglethorpe, Georgia. I worked for both the Red Food grocery store as well as a local bowling alley. I found myself in a tight dilemma: I had to pass an English class to graduate my senior year. The teacher,

Mrs. Marsh, gave me an assignment to write something about my life and how it helped me get to where I was today. I contacted my father and asked him if he thought it would be okay to write about him and Mr. Griffin. He said yes.

I wrote about the Battle of New Guinea and explained how my father had saved the future Governor's life in that battle. The teacher read my paper in front of the entire class, and then she began to question whether it was fiction or fact. In the end, she gave me a low grade, which kept me from passing. I contacted my father and asked his advice; he said, "Let me make a call." The next day, Mrs. Griffin contacted me and asked for the school's number and the name of my teacher.

Little did I realize what would happen next. I was sitting in class when an announcement came over: "Mrs. Marsh, you have an important call in the office."

I thought to myself, "Could it be?"

A short time passed and she returned to the class; she sat down for a minute and then stood up. "Class," she said, "the other day I read Marvin's paper to all of you, and I gave him a low grade because I did not realize that it could be true. I have now talked to the former Governor personally and know it's very true." She apologized to me and changed my grade so I could pass. I have never forgotten that experience.

I graduated high school in June 1979 and continued to work as a night stock manager at the Red Food store.

# CHAPTER 2

## Headed to the Army

An Army Recruiter in the local area contacted me over and over again. Finally he convinced me that the Army was the way to go, since I had no idea what the road ahead was. I entered active duty from Flintstone, Georgia, in April 1980. By midsummer I was in the heat of Fort Benning, Georgia, training to be an infantryman. I had an open contract, so I envisioned going to Airborne School and Ranger School fresh out of training, like many of my friends. Unfortunately, fate had a different idea.

I was extremely motivated to succeed, so I pushed myself each and every time to finish ahead of the pack. I remember the day so well when I was climbing down a rope at Fort Benning. The Drill Sergeant screamed, "Get down the damn rope!" For some reason, I did just that; unfortunately, it was the wrong way. I released my hands and fell to the ground, not realizing what had happened, and the adrenalin was flowing. I jumped up and ran over to my rucksack. Within several minutes, we were on the road headed back; as we began walking, I remember being tired; my ankles and feet were hurting more than usual for that period of training.

I don't recall much after that, except that I woke up in Martin Army Community Hospital with two broken ankles. I was hurting but was also worried that I would be recycled and not graduate. I had already been there more than enough for my liking. Drill Sergeant Walls came to visit me; he was a very good Drill Sergeant. He asked, "How are you doing, Private?"

I explained, "Well, I just want to get back to training."

He said, "Take your time and get better. I will take care of you."

The next day, I had crutches and was off to my unit; they put me on quarters so I still missed training. Fortunately for me, I was an 11H Anti-Armor Crewman, and the training was for 11B Infantrymen, so I didn't miss anything.

The time for the final Army Physical Fitness Test (APFT) came quicker than I could get healed. The Drill Sergeant said, "Rhodes, you can't take the Army Physical Fitness Test."

I replied, "Drill Sergeant, I can pass it, I am sure."

Drill Sergeant Walls said, "Okay, I will let you take it, but don't hurt yourself."

The next day, I woke up, tightened up my ankle supports, and got fired up. I breezed through the events and then the final challenge: the two-mile run in boots. Drill Sergeant Walls came up to me and said, "Rhodes, you amaze me. Just go out there and do your best. Don't hurt yourself."

The first lap, I found myself in the top ten, running like the wind. Drill Sergeant Walls was smiling and screaming, "Go, Rhodes, go!"

I finished with the third fastest time of the day. Drill Sergeant Walls used me as an example to other platoons, saying, "Even my broke private can run faster than you 'Joes'" (a term of endearment to us privates).

My career took shape from that point, and before I realized it, I was headed to Fort Campbell, Kentucky. Within nine months, I became the Battalion and Brigade Soldiers of the Quarter: the top Soldier for that period. I was the runner-up for the Fort Campbell Installation.

In 1982, I departed Fort Campbell and went to Friedberg, Germany. I had never been far from home, so I was enchanted when I arrived at my barracks by the twenty-foot ceilings from the old war caserns and the fact that no Soldiers were there. They had been alerted that morning to go to the border.

My career went by so fast from that point that I continued to excel and received numerous awards and decorations. None meant more than the day in 2002 when I had to choose. The Army selected me to attend the U.S. Army Sergeant Majors Academy. I had been a committed Soldier all those years, so I realized that in the coming months, something was going to occur, and I wanted to be a part of it. I informed the Department of the Army that my preference was to go to a unit that would deploy instead of to the academy. The Army enrolled me in distance learning so I could be reassigned. In November 2002, that wish came sooner than I expected. I was promoted to Sergeant Major (SGM) and reported to Fort Polk, Louisiana. Upon arrival, I was assigned to Third Squadron, Second Armored Cavalry Regiment (ACR); two months later, I was notified of my selection to CSM. That would take a while to reach.

# CHAPTER 3

## Road to War

I was selected to be the advance party Regimental Operations SGM; we departed in April and headed to Kuwait. I felt right at home; I had been to Kuwait before and knew well the surroundings. It made it simple to adjust.

My first priority was ensuring that I had a place where all our Soldiers could rest and prepare to cross the Line of Departure into Iraq. I was, of course, anxious. I remembered all too well those stories from my father and the former Governor about the loss of their friends and the impact that it made on them. I started writing more and more every day, thinking that it was a good possibility that I would become a casualty based on the estimated loss of life from the initial surge into Iraq. The main body arrived, and we were preparing to unload the ship that brought all our vehicles and equipment when we received a call from a Soldier who we left at the camp: "Sir, the tents are on fire. We're trying to put the fire out but the ammunition is going off."

Yes, we made some dumb decisions, placing ammunition in living areas with weapons. By the time we returned, about six tents had been destroyed and 250 Soldiers had lost all or part of their gear, including the Command Group, Squadron Commander, Command Sergeant Major, and critical staff.

I had been trained throughout my career to just get things done, so I immediately visited the local Army exchange that was on the camp. I talked to the manager and told them what had occurred. The idea was to make each Soldier comfortable with a blanket, pillow, and personal hygiene items for the night. I did just that.

The next morning, I received a call to come to the Regimental Tactical Operations Center (TOC). "SGM, did you authorize the purchase of $20,000-plus of gear for Soldiers?"

I was shocked and asked myself, "Why am I being asked this question?"

I replied, "Roger that, Sir." A few more words passed and I continued the mission at hand. I figured a smart person would figure it all out. It was never mentioned to me again.

We crossed the border headed to Iraq; I was the advance party again. How sweet is that? At least there won't be any surprises. We crossed the border and knew that some poor hungry locals might try to take our gear. We tied everything down, and rehearsed by using sticks instead of bullets to warn them off.

We arrived in Iraq; it was a normal setting, which I had become accustomed to rather easily. I was amazed by the children and saddened by the way they had to live. As we got closer to Baghdad, I could see that "the rich got richer" mentality certainly worked well here.

On May 23, 2003, I had a life-altering encounter: an attack on our base camp. Someone screamed out as the power went off.

The rooftop guard had been injured; a fellow Soldier and I rushed to the roof. Everyone was so worried about second and third attacks that it took a moment to assess the area before getting to the wounded Soldier. He was shot through one side and out the other. We stabilized him and carried him down.

This was just the beginning for me. I was traumatized, not knowing what to think, and instinctively I started barking out orders, giving directions to secure the camp. We had only been there for a day, so we had not done a complete assessment to ensure the security was tight.

I had to make a decision at that point: be scared, be afraid, show weakness, or just harden up and accomplish the mission. I showed no remorse, no concern for the wounded Soldier, I just echoed, "See what I have told you? Stay situationally aware all the time."

Who is our enemy? Everyone is. I repeated that same thing over and over again until I felt they understood it. Over the next fifteen months of OIF 1 and 2, we would encounter the enemy at every angle. Mortar attacks, rocket attacks, small arms fire, and IEDs. I had just been promoted to Regimental Operations SGM when I wrote several letters to the families of the twenty-three Soldiers with me. I then decided that some of these Soldiers were way too experienced to be there and needed to be down at the squadron level. That decision almost cost a Soldier his life. I told SPC Green, "You're going to a squadron; pack your bags." Yes, I told him why: "Career enhancement, you're senior," all the standard stuff.

Two days later on a patrol, his vehicle was hit with an IED. He was not seriously wounded but I left the Forward Operating Base (FOB) immediately to go to the Combat Support Hospital. When I arrived, I found him in good spirits; I looked at him as I held his hand and thought, "Did I cause this?"

He looked as if he knew what I was thinking. He said, "SGM, it's not your fault. I volunteered for this patrol. You were right, all these guys are too new to be down here."

I felt relieved. I left the room and walked around and talked to numerous Soldiers, one Soldier worried about his buddy, another Soldier just happy to be alive. That was the norm throughout the hospital. I was extremely blessed. The sights and sounds of this hospital left me challenged at night. I found myself unable to sleep. When I did sleep, I would sleepwalk and wake up wondering how I got to where I was. One day, we heard explosions so we climbed to the roof of our sleeping quarters to see how far away it was. It was several miles away but so huge that we thought it was right outside the FOB.

That night turned out to be a turning point for me. I didn't realize that the malaria pills I had been taking could cause side effects, one of which was a mode-altering disorder that could lead to sleepwalking. I relived the day's events and sleepwalked to the top of the building. I awoke to my displeasure on the top of that building; I was scared and wondered how I had gotten there.

The next morning, I went to see the physician's assistant and told him what had occurred. He diagnosed that the medicine probably had caused it and I should stop taking it; this had not been my first encounter with sleepwalking. I immediately began tying my leg to the cot that I slept on. I also put stuff up against the door to keep me from exiting during the nights in which I didn't tie myself up.

The attack that followed would continue to haunt me later in my career. I remember all too well the attack on the United Nations building; the Executive Officer for the regiment called me and said, "The 72 wants you there now." I arrived to one of the worst scenes of death and destruction that I have ever seen in my life. The UN Ambassador was still alive under the rubble; later, we would find out that he made a call to get help but later died. The people in the immediate blast area were covered with glass, and many died. We secured the area and established a perimeter. About two days later, my driver and I were headed to the UN area; just up ahead, a matter of eight seconds away, a vehicle exploded, killing several Iraq police.

I never imagined how close death and destruction had come to me since I arrived in the Middle East in April 2003; I was speechless, to say the least. As a leader, I remained calm, cool, and collected in public. I spent many days discussing with the chaplain and friends how terrible some of these terrorist attacks had become. I had always appreciated life and the simple ways that it could pass you by. Certainly this wasn't any different than losing a friend or relative back home.

Each day we had been in country, we observed death. One day, my Soldiers and I were driving down Canal Street when we came upon two bodies in the middle of the road. They had been killed the night before. We didn't realize why or what message was being sent by putting them in the middle of the street. We just remained quiet; each Soldier in my patrol had his own thoughts going on. I could see it in their faces. I realized as death came closer how precious life really was; in some ways, I began to realize how I was changing a little each day. I began not calling home as much, I had less desire to write (with the exception of writing home to my soldiers' families to let them know how they were doing; I made efforts on numerous occasions to write their families).

A short while after my first letter, I received an email from a mom. Usually, they would write, "Sir," not "Sergeant Major." You know, we enlisted folks sometimes joke, "I am not a 'sir,' I work for living." Having spent most of my twenty-nine years in the military as a leader at some level, I have grown to love officers. They truly desire to lead Soldiers both in combat and at home as we prepare for what's next. Officers are generally educated and think differently than enlisted Soldiers. On one hand, I think about how to get things done quickly without regard for what happens after. An officer, from my experience through the development process, always has a better understanding of where this goes next. A vision of sorts. Yes, enlisted Soldiers use their hands to work for a living. The officers work just as hard with their minds. It's a team effort; we can't move forward one without the other.

The letter simply stated, "Thanks for the letter. My son is SPC Jones and he hasn't written or called in several months." Instantly, I got the message. I notified the platoon sergeant to have this Soldier come visit me in the Regimental Tactical Operation Center. He arrived a short while after; I asked him to sit down and started the conversation with, "Tell me a little bit about yourself."

The Soldier begin telling me about where he joined the Army and how long he had been in. I always like using signs and gestures to communicate. As he continued to speak about the Army, I placed my index finger over my lips to indicate, "Okay, I got it." I asked him an easy question: "Are you married?"

He replied, no, he lived with his mom and dad.

I jokingly said, "I got two beautiful daughters," and I showed him their picture. I had him confused. A Sergeant Major doesn't spend a lot of time talking about family. He was wondering where I was going. Then I said, "How is your Mom doing?"

I could see the amazement on his face. We talked a little about my own father and mom and how I had failed miserably over my career to stay in contact with them, forgetting how I got here and what impact they had on my life. I didn't say, "Go write your family."

About two weeks later, I got a thank-you note from his mom. She said, "I don't know what you said to my son but I have gotten three letters this week."

That gave me the desire to keep writing. I wrote hundreds of letters since that date to parents as well as to my hometown newspaper about where we were in the Iraq War.

The one thing I lost from this was my own sense of importance; I recognized that I had to remain focused and situationally aware at all times. I developed a sixth sense to second-guess what we were doing and provided my advice and recommendations to the leaders above me to help us through the combat tour, which was extended in April 2004 to July 2004. I remember this day so clearly, like it happened yesterday. I was sitting in the Tactical Operations Center; First Cavalry was to relieve us on April 4, 2004; about an hour before the change, a unit came under fire in Sadr City in Baghdad.

"We are receiving small arms fire," the initial message said, but we realized there were multiple engagements. The enemy surprised us that day. I can't say a lot about this. When it was all said and done, we lost eight Soldiers and over fifty-five wounded in just a few hours. It was one of the largest dust-offs that occurred since the Iraq War began. I begin to think, "We're not going anywhere, we're staying longer." All my Soldiers were excited about going home. We even had Soldiers already on the way home. I still remained calm, with no desire to go home, only wanting to remain in contact. To me, this had become my home, for now. As we travel throughout our careers in the Army, we adjust to our location and know that within a couple years, we will be going to another place. This time, I didn't feel that, I felt we needed to stay, this is where we're needed. We have a lot to do.

I received the word from the operations officer that I was to move and establish the Tactical Operations Center and another Forward Operating Base in preparation to stage the regiment's move to the Najaf area of Iraq. I became instantly motivated. We're staying. I was excited; others simple got overwhelmed in the moment but not me. I began barking out orders and letting Soldiers know what to do, where we were going, and so on.

The first night at the temporary FOB, we received a warm welcome from our closest friends: a mortar barrage. A Soldier ran into my sleep area and said, "SGM, we're under attack!"

I replied, "Okay, go back to sleep; it will be fine. Keep your helmet and sap vest on."

Inside I wondered, "Okay, I hope they got this FOB secured." I already knew a patrol would automatically head toward the area they fired from. We would counterattack, but running from a firing location was a simple process for the enemy. More often than not, we wouldn't get any battle damage from counterfire.

Three days later, I got some more good news: "SGM, the Division wants you to lead the first patrol south. Whoa! You're taking forty vehicles with you!"

"What, whose stupid idea was that?" I thought.

Minutes later, I would find out: "SGM, the DCG Tactical Operations Center and his security will be in your convoy."

I was stunned. Not only did I have to worry about my Soldiers, now I had someone else to worry about. I briefed the entire patrol and made sure everyone knew the route, and knew what actions to take on contact. There was always guesswork, such as what happens if we get hit at the front of the convoy? Okay, I got that; I was the second vehicle in the patrol. I felt that was the likely vehicle they would hit, and I felt I could react well enough to that and still remain in control of the convoy. What about the middle or the back? I placed key folks throughout the convoy I knew could handle the pressure of attacks. We took off on the convoy; everything went smoothly for the first twenty kilometers or so.

We took a short halt to rest and regain our focus. About fifteen minutes later, we moved out again.

Approximately five minutes later, I heard a pop. Instantly, the gunner from the lead vehicle opened fire. The gunner, SPC Harris, was the man in my book that day; he probably single-handedly saved the convoy. As I heard the pop and the machine-gun fire opened up, I turned and watched as an RPG went over my vehicle. Simultaneously, I watched SPC Harris remove the enemy as an obstacle. As I turned and watched the RPG go over my vehicle, I observed out of the corner of my eye another RPG to my front; this time, it seemed certain it was going to hit us. But for some reason, it went over my truck and hit the truck behind me. The vehicle was damaged, but like many RPGs, it didn't explode. The driver was hurt.

I immediately observed a truck with ten to twelve armed insurgents approaching us from the west at a face pace. It was like in a movie; I opened fire with my M4; SPC Harris and several others began firing as well. That was a good day for the home team; when it was all said and done, we killed twelve insurgents that day and survived an RPG barrage. We continued up the road and did another short halt. A call came from the rear that all had cleared the engagement area and all was good. We continued to the camp in the south.

The next day, I got a call to come to the TOC. The DCG from First Armored Division had arrived and he had received the report. His team credited me and my security team for getting them there safely. He thanked me; "Roger, Sir." He told me if I needed anything to let him know. I acknowledged and continued. A close call nonetheless with death.

As we continued our three-month extension, I became more and more engaged with the enemy, attempting to win hearts and minds. I worked with on humanitarian aid projects to help the locals. My team visited areas where it appeared that no one had gone to in a while. As we talked to the local schoolmaster, he showed us what he needed to educate the children in the region as well as to improve the school's condition. It was horrible; the summers were hot in Iraq. When we arrived, the classrooms had no windows and no air-conditioning. I discussed it with the headmaster and assured him that we would help.

I talked to the unit, and before we knew it, we started receiving school supplies and even CERP funds to help rebuild this school. The headmaster was excited; through my interpreter, he thanked me for what Second Squadron, Eleventh Armored Cavalry Regiment was doing. He said this helped but he needed this, that, and the other. "Will you meet with our community leaders to discuss?" I said okay and scheduled a day to meet. The next day, a patrol was coming by the school to FOB Duke, where we had established a new home, and was hit by an IED across the road from the school.

When I received the report, I immediately became angry. I called for my patrol security team and said, "Let's go." I headed out to the school; I was so angry. When I arrived, only the headmaster was at the school. I told the interpreter, "Ask him who did this?"

He asked the headmaster, who was very reluctant to say anything. He finally got the message: "Unless you help me, I am not helping you anymore, no water line, no second school up the road, and no more food every two days or so."

He finally told us that some strangers from another area had taken up a site about two clicks off the road. We searched and searched the area, with no luck. I informed the headmaster of the school, "One more attack and we stop everything." The remaining three months were quiet in that area.

This tour took a toll on the regiment: twenty-one regimental troopers lost their lives in Iraq. The deaths of these warriors weighed heavily on my heart as we got closer and closer to coming back to the States. Yes, I had stopped thinking about home many months before, only seeing it as a return from where my fellow Soldiers gave their all. One Soldier, in particular, I met while in Iraq. Eric Cook was a friend of the regimental CSM; we would get together on occasion, with other Sergeant Majors, and talk; think about the good times. On one such occasion in the middle of December 2003, we did just that; little did I realize that one of us would be taken soon.

I was resting in my room on the day before Christmas; the night was closing. A knock came to the door; I always keep myself ready to respond to anything. The knock came loudly; the voice outside was the regimental CSM, who said, "Eric Cook just got killed by an IED."

My heart seemed to stop for a moment; I couldn't imagine that here was a brigade-level CSM, who loved Soldiers, who had been taken from us. I got up immediately and went to the TOC; I listened as the radio reports came through. Nothing about Eric. It seemed like the longest night we would have. The next day, Christmas, December 25, 2003, I just stayed to myself. I tried to clear my mind but I couldn't. The chaplain came by and talked but I really wasn't in the mood for listening. I just couldn't understand.

The pain from the loss of every Soldier whose memorial I attended was special; I tried to celebrate their life and put a positive spin on it when talking to their Soldiers. When I was alone, I would find myself becoming more and more emotional. Some people say it's okay to cry; I hope so, because I needed to do just that—a lot. As the tour came to an end, I knew that I wanted to stay. Many regimental Soldiers felt the same way. However, we are soldiers; we go where we are told, and we do just that. However, the one advantage of being a Sergeant Major, you sometimes get a vote. I contact the SGM Branch and worked my way back to Georgia. During the process, I was selected as command Sergeant Major but had to wait to get a battalion. I worked my way on the staff of one of the finest officers in this man's Army: Lieutenant General Steven Whitcomb, then the Commander of Third U.S. Army.

# CHAPTER 4

## Feeling the Loss One by One

I lost six Soldiers since we deployed here in January 2005. In early April, we started into a new phase of our ongoing operation. That was when the deaths of my Soldiers quickly went from zero to six in just twenty-four days, with almost two dozen wounded. The enemy had to get a vote, and they did.

I took it hard, to say the least; anytime one of my great Soldiers gives his life for the purposes of a better tomorrow, it is truly the ultimate sacrifice.

Since we continued to attack the enemy in hopes of a brighter tomorrow, we are not discouraged whatsoever. Most of my Soldiers merely see the loss of these great American Soldiers as part of God's will to continue the fight. We of course have our questions about why. However, as Soldiers, as Americans, we have to understand that there is a greater purpose, and we will be successful in all that we do.

We endured the loss of two Company Commanders, both with children, each oth with a wonderful young wife waiting at home and supporting their every need in this war as well as looking after other soldiers' spouses, even in their sadness for the loss of their husbands.

We have a great country; a lot of individuals want to continue to make life tough for the Iraqi people through the killing of innocent children and Iraqis, who only want their god to allow them the opportunity for another tomorrow. They live for tomorrow; they celebrate life and cherish it. They continue to celebrate birthdays, holidays, and even weddings with joy and enthusiasm like there is no war.

In the past two years, I have learned a lot about the customs of the people we are trying to provide some constructive organization and a democratic environment. They are for the most part looking forward to the opportunity to have a peaceful country.

Some of them see what Kuwait is now and credit that to the U.S. Army. I would say we provided the basics of a peaceful environment; they provided the well.

As the days go by, we see the news, just like you in the States; we see our fellow Marines being killed, and we hear their families talk. Most of them say what we all really think: "He died doing what he believed in. He died because he wanted a better future for Iraq."

It's not Iraq that we are fighting here anymore; I drive all over this country, and I see smiling faces and barefoot kids waving and smiling. I see men and women giving a broken smile and hoping that the insurgents are not around.

Yes, today we are at war. However, just like our Veterans from the past, we too will be successful in this endeavor.

My question is, what's next, and which country will we have to help see the error in their ways? The Iraqi Army Soldiers have told me time and time again, "I will go with the American Army to any country to fight beside them." This is a great compliment to our Soldiers, as well as to all Americans. Yes, we are not without our issues, with Social Security and so on.

After being a part of this operation here in Iraq over the last three years, since April 2003, I find myself the resident expert about a lot of things. The day-to-day business as usual is different for me based on my current experience level compared to those around me. As the heat started rising in May 2005, the Soldiers would stop talking normally; most of them would begin their conversation with, "CSM, it sure is hot."

I would reply almost every time with, "Soldier, you better be drinking water; it's not hot yet." They would leave and say, "HOOAH, CSM." I knew, having been in Iraq for the previous two summers, that the heat would come in August, and then it would turn cold in September. Like our country, they have a consistent weather pattern.

Unfortunately, it's another election—another situation that I am well familiar with—coming upon us. It the time when the Coalition Forces will put up the strongest level of security that anyone has ever seen. Again we will bury some American service members as a result of the increased security and the enemy's increased determination to have us fail. Yes, I see the way ahead, and I truly see the light at the end of the tunnel. Most Soldiers, over the next three months, will experience the challenge of their lifetime. Their dreams will come and go, thinking only of tomorrow and the hopes that there will be one.

A fellow American, Carl Carroll, a retired Chief Warrant Officer 4 working for the Titan Company, was killed after departing my FOB to go to Baghdad. This was and remains a tough thing for me to swallow. A lot of Americans do not realize that we service members cannot do our job without the support of companies like Titan and Halliburton. They have given us a quality of life that most Soldiers only dream about. The quality of life is unprecedented in previous wars. Still, we have service members who do not realize that their fellow Veterans before us did not have these luxuries. I for one appreciate all Americans who have volunteered to come into harm's way and support our troops.

To the lady who lost a son, who continues to attack the President in his hometown and other places, I say to her, "I for one feel the pain of a lost Soldier, I have now personally experienced the loss of thirty-four Soldiers and one civilian directly in the unit that I was assigned. Yes, you are an American. Yes, you have the right to speak out. Is this not how the backlash of the Vietnam War started? Over 2,000 service members in the Coalition have lost their lives in support of establishing freedom for this country. Look at American history. Think before you react, thousands and thousands of families lost their fathers and sons during past wars. Their sacrifice has made our country the best nation in this world. So, please remember your son for what he did and honor him by letting him rest in peace."

Finally, I would like the Ringgold paper to take one page and place the pictures of all the great service members, regardless of service, who have paid the ultimate price and extended their memory. I would like to see this especially for all our Georgia residents and Americans. This will be a great tribute to our great Soldiers. I suggest that we do this until the war is over and our troops come home.

May the best part of life come to all of you great Ringgold folks!

# CHAPTER 5

## Coming Home with a Lifetime of Memories

I arrived home late November 2005, but things were different for me. I constantly thought about losing the sixteen warriors in combat, plus Carl Carroll, a retired aviation Veteran who came to Iraq to assist as a civilian. We had become very close; one morning, I can't recall exactly what I was doing, but I heard a loud explosion in the area outside of Forward Operating Base. I immediately contacted the Tactical Operation Center and asked them what was going on. They responded, "The Special Forces patrol was hit with an IED attack; one vehicle is on fire." I immediately went to the TOC to see what was going on. I got a situation update that reflected one civilian was being brought to our Troop Medical Clinic (TMC). I went to the TMC and Carl arrived; I watched every second as our great medical staff, led by Dr. Bean, worked diligently to save him. They announced he was gone a short while later.

I remember ever so clearly the thoughts that ran through my mind that day: Am I ready? Have I done everything to ensure my family is taken care of? Before that day, I had gone on hundreds of patrols. When we first arrived in this area, the top three leaders' patrols were hit almost daily, with little damage. The Squadron Commander even told me, "CSM, slow down, I need you." "Roger, sir," I said. "When you slow down, I will." He laughed. He was a great ambassador for our soldiers; his passion for ensuring they were taken care of as well as maintaining contact with the enemy left us in great shape for almost a hundred days before we lost our first warrior, PFC LaWare.

I returned home to a huge welcome home party; the neighbors, my cousins, and others came to see me. I was relatively happy. Still in my stomach I was sick, sick that I had made it through thirty months of combat. Many more did not; I can see their faces in my mind all the time. I tried hard to stay busy, even cut short my vacation to report into my new position as the Brigade Command Sergeant Major, for the Basic Combat Training Brigade at Fort Benning, Georgia. I was excited, sharing my experiences with these Soldiers and leaders to help better prepare them for what was next in their lives. Colonel Charles W. Durr had interviewed me by phone several months back and was willing to wait for me to return. He said, "It's just that important to have the most recently experienced CSM to advise me."

As I took the job, I found myself forgetting about the war unless I met up with friends and fellow warriors, or I would watch the TV, which I chose not to do very often.

I remember when I first arrived, the good Commander told me, "CSM, see you at Building 4."

"What for, sir?" I asked.

"Oh, we spend a lot of time there on briefings, ceremonies, and luncheons."

I had been given a government vehicle to drive, so I left about twenty minutes early in order to reach the meeting on time.

I had been a Drill Sergeant at Fort Benning from 1989 to 1992, so I knew the area well already, but some changes had occurred. I left Sand Hill and headed to go down Dixie Road at Harmony Church then headed on in toward Building 4. As I cleared the main area and headed down the last straightaway on Dixie Road, gunfire rang out. My heart almost stopped; I jerked my steering wheel and quickly gathered myself to realize it was just range firing. I took a deep breath and said to myself, "I got to find a new route." I was constantly changing routines so as not to spend a majority of my time focusing on the past, unless I got emails, letters, or even phone calls from past friends or fellow warriors who needed me. As I visited ranges more and more, I found that I had to find time to visit these Soldiers when they were not firing; to be honest, there wasn't a lot I could do to help them or even talk to them when they were that engaged.

I talked to the Commander about setting up different venues to see the Soldiers, in briefs, quarterly cadre briefs, and even cycle briefs from individual companies, to stay on top of the training and to stay engaged with the Soldiers and leaders alike. This minimized my contact with live fire ranges.

About thirty days into the position, I was tasked to go to Atlanta for a couple of days to discuss what task and battle drills should be added or deleted for the new warrior task and battle drills the Army came up with. When the Commander told me this, I looked at him and asked, "Sir, what the hell is warrior task and battle drills?"

I had been at war so long that the Army had become smarter and created this.

I arrived in Atlanta the morning of the meeting, instead of leaving the day before; I hated traveling. I hated being alone. It was the toughest time that I would have. Being alone and having time to think has been my worst enemy for the last several years. It remains that to this day.

I meet Colonel Shwedo, the G-3 for the Army accessions command; we talked a minute or so, and the discussions began. I sat patiently, as all good CSM do, listening to each word but thinking, "Okay, genius, where is your combat patch if you know so damn much?"

After a while, it came to me. Our discussion had been about the tasks they thought were important and how we could create what they called white space by deleting the tasks that weren't important.

I started off slowly and said, "Look, call for fire is important, but not for Basic Training Soldiers." Their eyes peaked. I added, "Crew served weapons are important as well, but unless they're driving down the road engaging targets, then that too is a task for their next duty station."

Finally, I came to the task that was really heavy on my heart. While I was in combat on numerous occasions, my patrols would come across other patrols that had been hit with IEDs.

That was the easy part, giving the situation; the hard part was trying to understand why they didn't know a damn thing about combat lifesaver tasks and how to apply the four basic lifesaving measures. One time, a patrol was hit; they were escorting a fuel truck to another FOB in our area. As we drove up, the rear seat was heavily damaged and a Soldier leaned across the seat, bleeding from shrapnel. My patrol immediately secured the area and rendered first aid to that Soldier. From that time, I constantly reinforced first aid training for first responders.

I talk briefly about the above and emphasized that the most important thing we're very good at is taking the fight to the enemy and destroying them at will. We are a failure at providing the necessary first response first aid to our Soldiers, that's why they die of the wounds received. Colonel Shwedo jumped on that quickly, and it instantly became the theme of Tradoc to ensure all Soldiers left initial military training as a combat lifesaver. It has made a huge difference to date.

The first year went by quickly, and I was again tasked to go to Fort Jackson for a two-week Pre-Command Course for CSM/COL. The Thursday prior to departing for Fort Jackson, I woke up in severe pain. I didn't know what it was. Like every day, I got up, put on my physical fitness clothes, and headed to work. That morning, I just moved a little slower.

I got to work at almost the same time as the Commander that morning; I was lucky he had not parked at the same time as me. I moved slowly up the stairs to the office and sat at my desk on the second floor, still in pain. The good Colonel and I ran all the time together; he had become my battle buddy; I shared almost everything in my life with him, except that I had been diagnosed with PTSD. I regret that to this date. He approached my door and said, "CSM, it's Thursday; time for a long run."

I said, "Sir, not today."

He left for the run. I went next door to the TMC to see what the hell was going on. They said, "You got rocks in your bladder and they are trying to come out." They sent me to the hospital for an MRI, but on the way, I couldn't wait and went to the restroom in the hospital. By the time I got to the MRI, I was already feeling better.

When I was done, they said no running for two weeks. Well, I would try.

I departed Sunday for Fort Jackson and arrived, checked in, and went to my room. The next morning, I remember so clearly waking up. I had watched TV the day before, and it was all about what was going on in Iraq and how more troops were dying. It left a heavy load on my heart before I went to sleep. That night, I woke screaming; I remember my wife at the time telling me that I couldn't understand how I lived and these young Soldiers had died.

I began sleepwalking again; I had to resort back to tying my leg to the bed with my boot string to prevent me from going anywhere. Now I have a sleep apnea machine that is strapped to my head and blows air all night into my nose. It's very uncomfortable, but it keeps me alive.

# CHAPTER 6

## The Death of a Best Friend's Son

I would like to take a few moments to share some thoughts on the patriotism of our great country as it relates to Ringgold, Georgia, and a town I was saddened to visit this last weekend in Kentucky.

As the Soldier's Creed says, "I am a warrior and a member of a team, I will never leave a fallen comrade." That was never more true than at a funeral I attended on Saturday, September 30, 2006, in Loudon, Kentucky, for SFC Jason Jones.

On Thursday, September 21, 2006, I received a call that a good friend of mine had passed away; as with most messages, the first report is almost every time wrong. I was emotionally drained by the time I realized that this information was inadequate. Unfortunately, it was worse than I could imagine.

Colonel Charlie Jones, a friend and fellow warrior, deployed to Iraq last spring with his twenty-nine-year-old son Jason with him. The message was informing me that Colonel Jones's son had died on September 21, 2006, while defending our country in Iraq. Unfortunately, the message was incomplete and just said a good friend had died in Iraq.

Colonel Charlie Jones is one of the best Soldiers I have ever served with in my twenty-six-year career in the U.S. Army. I contacted Colonel Jones after he returned from Iraq on Saturday, September 23, 2006. To say the least, I was tongue-tied to start our conversation about the death of his son.

After a few minutes, a great conversation evolved, in which I grew up about ten years from his words.

He acknowledged the great American Soldier that his son was during his Army career and his willingness to put his life into harm's way for our country. It was, to say the least, a blessing for me to hear that from him first-hand. This man had just made the ultimate sacrifice, his son, to our cause, freedom.

Too many of our fellow Americans have chosen not to support the war effort that our country has undertaken. I challenge them to take a moment and recognize the huge sacrifice that all our service members make daily on their behalf.

On September 30, my wife Carol and I proceeded from Fort Benning, Georgia, to Loudon, Kentucky, the longest journey I had taken in a while. This journey was in some ways tougher than my trip to Iraq on three separate occasions.

It's tough enough to drive these days and remain focused on the roads and the other drivers, but this day was tougher. I had not seen my friend since my deployment to Iraq in 2003. We were in constant contact by email over the last three years, and he had called my wife on several occasions to make sure she was doing well while I was deployed.

This death brought back the memories of the numerous memorials that I attended in Iraq, for my Soldiers as well as fellow Soldiers of other units. These memories are the worst part of fighting for our country. You try to shake them by staying busy and occupied. Then another great American Soldier dies in Iraq or Afghanistan, and then the thoughts come full circle. As my days go by, I drive down some of our roads at Fort Benning, and loud explosions and gunfire ring out. I have to take a deep breath, as it is all too similar to real war.

Carol knows all too well that every Soldier's death has affected my heart, and these Soldiers fighting for our country mean more to me than anything.

We arrived about ninety minutes early, took a moment to remember Jason, and walked outside. I was excited to see approximately 500 bikers with American flags. Who were these people? They were Patriotguard Riders from Kentucky and the surrounding region.

They had mobilized to defend our American hero's honor and to prevent those who wanted to protest from dishonoring him. I sat in amazement and said, "I need to thank every one of these folks." As I reached out my hand to the first man, my eyes watered. I could barely contain my inner thoughts of how proud I was to be amongst these patriot saints.

I started at the front and walked my way through the crowd of bikers.

I am sure all of our fallen comrades, resting quietly, looked down that day; as we completed the funeral and stood at the cemetery, a slight rain began to fall. Carol leaned over and said, "Babe, the angels are crying with happy tears today."

I could not imagine what our American society thought; until this funeral, I had become discouraged by recent media talk, but the following things made me feel pleased:

- The number of people who attended the funeral and the number of people who just came and stood outside the funeral home, showing the American flag in support of this Fallen Soldier.

- A Gold Star mother, with the daughter of a deceased Soldier, paying homage to Charlie's son. What a painful memory that must have been to her, yet you could see she was so proud of her kid. She was there to support the Joneses.

- The professionalism of the local and state police, who provided security and controlled traffic, and the respect they paid to a fallen solder as the procession wound its way to the cemetery.

- The citizens of Kentucky who pulled over on the side on the road as the funeral procession went past. They could have kept driving, but they chose not to.

- The number of people stopping their lawn work to pay respect to the funeral procession that passed by.

- The Governor of Kentucky, who sat in a pew very inconspicuously but was there to support the family.

- The bikers and other supporters who by their sheer numbers blocked out the view of the protestors. You knew the protestors only showed up because our beloved media thought it was important you know about this frivolous protest.

- The professionalism of the Kentucky National Guard Soldiers and their leaders: how they took care of the family, the conduct of the twenty-one-gun salute, "Taps," and the helicopter fly-over.

- A mother out on the front porch in Keavy, Kentucky, saluting every car as it passed by with American flags waving. "Why did she do this?" I wondered. Seems to me she either has a son over there or knows what it means to sacrifice, or maybe she is just a great American.

- A young boy with a crew cut, about nine or ten years old, holding a hand over his heart as the procession neared the cemetery.

Some of these thoughts are from a fellow warrior who served with me; yes, I borrowed them to explain some of my feelings and ensure I captured the essence of patriotism.

Loudon, Kentucky, reminded me of Ringgold, Georgia. When I came back to Ringgold three years ago on a regular basis, we saw the flags of all our great service members who are no longer with us.

One of them is for my father, who served our country proudly.

These flags stand in honor of these great soldiers; I am happy to say there is at least one other city with this attitude in America, and I am sure now that there are many more.

I am satisfied now that patriotism is alive and well, despite the critics. As the funeral ended, I had several hours to reflect with my friend. As we talked, I told Charlie of my anger that the protestors had come.

Charlie replied, "Sam, it just tells me that what we are doing is right."

I paused with amazement. Then I said, "Charlie, I wish just one of them would confront me directly."

He replied, "That's a horse of a different color." I knew exactly what that meant.

I knew then this great Soldier was doing well; his thoughts were easing, despite the loss of his only son and his upcoming return to combat. I know his heart will be always with Jason, but his mind was with his troops in Iraq.

He was excited about returning and completing his mission and bringing the remainder of his troops home safely.

Please continue to support our troops and pray for them often; it's these American heroes who are giving us the opportunity to sleep through the night without worry.

I, for one, am proud to say "I'm an American."

# CHAPTER 7

## Veterans Day

What is the purpose of Veterans Day? I thought about this on November 11, 2008, as I celebrated with my family and the first-grade class of New Mountain Hill, Fortson, Georgia. I did some research to find our more information before I began to share my thoughts. I found thousands of words, but done more important than those of our former President:

## THE WHITE HOUSE OFFICE

## October 8, 1954

I have today signed a proclamation calling upon all of our citizens to observe Thursday, November 11, 1954 as Veterans Day. It is my earnest hope that all Veterans, their organizations, and the entire citizenry will join hands to insure proper and widespread observance of this day". With the thought that it will be most helpful to coordinate the planning, I am suggesting the formation of a Veterans Day National Committee. In view of your great

personal interest as well as your official responsibil-
ities, I have designated you to serve as Chairman.
You may include in the Committee membership
such other persons as you desire to select and I am
requesting the heads of all departments and agen-
cies of the Executive branch to assist the Committee
in its work in every way possible.

I have every confidence that our Nation will respond wholeheartedly in the appropriate observance of Veterans Day, 1954.

Sincerely,

DWIGHT D. EISENHOWER

Yes, it was the earnest hope of Dwight D. Eisenhower that our nation would respond whole-heartedly in the observance of Veterans
Day. They have, but is it enough? I was asked by my first-grade
grandson, Tanner Martin, to come and eat lunch with his class. I
was humbled by the invitation to his small-town school in rural
Fortson, Georgia, which asked Veterans to come for lunch. I arrived an hour early like all good Soldiers should. As I approached
the school, my throat tightened, and I felt anxious and ready to
cry. No, I wasn't unhappy; I was again overjoyed with happiness. I
entered the building and met the receptionist; she gave me a name
tag that said "Happy Veterans Day." It was already a wonderful
one; however, I didn't realize how wonderful it would get.

I was directed to Tanner's class to meet his teacher, Ms. Ellis;
I entered the class and started to remember how much I really

enjoyed the younger days of my schooling … "NOT!" I informed Ms. Ellis that I had brought a bag with some items for the kids: an American flag, candy, and a wrist band with the word "HOOAH" on it. The kids reluctantly heard that they were not to open the bag until after the reading period, which was coming up. I went with four kids to another classroom, where Mrs. Pate had us all sit on the floor in a circle; all the students read for about thirty minutes before they went to lunch.

I sat, quietly, watching the teacher interact with about fifteen kids; all of the kids were reading and were excited about answering the questions about the story. I was amazed, and then she got to the part about how animals would camouflage themselves in order to survive in their environment. Then I became the center of attention. The teacher said, "You see Tanner's grandfather's uniform?" They all said "Yes!" in harmony.

"What color is it?"

"Brown," they said.

"Where would you use that color if you wanted to hide from your enemies?"

They all said, so smart, "The desert."

I was getting involved. I thought, "Oh no, maybe I am supposed to be reading too!"

Reading time flew by so quickly.

Before I knew it, I was back in the classroom and taking photos with the kids and talking about some tokens that I had brought to share: dog tags that I wore in Iraq for three combat tours, for over thirty months. I had some other items as well. They asked many questions, some more direct than others.

Then it came time to open the bag of goodies that I brought for them. I was thinking to myself, "What will they pull out first?"

I should have guessed. It was the small American flag, they all pulled it out first. I had to get a photo. Then I was amazed again when they yelled out, "USA!"

Truly, this Veterans Day was a blessing so far. We finished up the moment with the bag and went straight to lunch; all the kids were trying to figure out how to sit with Tanner and his grandfather. They all had plenty of questions and wanted me to help them open something for them. I figured that they could have handled it themselves, but I opened milk cartons, snack stuff, and even some frozen peaches.

We spent about thirty minutes together at lunch and we had a great time; one boy told me his mom was in the Army, another one told me his grandfather was a Soldier but he died last year. Finally, the best part was when two boys and a little girl said, "I am going to be a Soldier."

I smiled, thinking, "Hopefully you will give your education a chance first."

So have we accomplished what President Dwight D. Eisenhower wanted for Veterans Day? Do you think we have? Unfortunately, across the country, the kids still have to go to school instead of spending the day with their Veteran.

All in all, it was truly a great Veterans Day for me!

God bless our greatest asset, our children!

# CHAPTER 8

## First Responder

I started my day off on June 13, 2009, 0700 with breakfast with my wife Cathy, and I prepared to head out to get a few workers to help me repair some fence for Ann Slaughter, a friend of ours. I drove to Columbus and picked up a few workers and headed to Ann's home, off Cannon Road in Harris County, just a few miles from our home. Her husband, John Slaughter, had passed away earlier in the year. I was driving down the road by her home one day and noticed that the fence that bordered her home, with a small lake in the center of it, was falling down. I dropped by to talk and introduced myself. Once I met her, I knew instantly that this was a terrific lady. I asked her if she would rent her pasture out to me to board a couple horses.

She replied, "My fence probably won't hold the horses."

I stated I would be more than glad to fix it for her if it we could work something out. She said fine. The next day was Saturday, so I got up early on my own and went and started repairing the fence. About two hours into fixing the fence, it started raining really bad. I kept working. Butch, her nephew, came out and asked if I wanted to come in to get dry. I said no thank you and continued to work. An hour or so later, it stopped raining and the most beautiful rainbow appeared. It was a beautiful day.

This was a different day, and the work was too much for me so I enlisted some helpers to help me put a big dent into it. We arrived around 9 AM and we started working, removing weeds and tree limbs and other stuff, in preparation to repair the fence. About three hours later, my wonderful wife, Cathy, brought us our lunch. We had lunch and worked for a few hours more. It was about 3:45 when I called it a day, and we drove down to the local fuel tech to get some cash out of the ATM to pay my workers. For some reason, the ATM didn't work for me; time and time before, it had worked for me.

I decided to drive back toward my home to the hardware store and see if Mr. Wilson could give me some cash through his machine. He provided me some cash and off I went. Little did I realize the purpose of this eight-minute delay in my travels. I drove toward Columbus, relaxing after a hard day's work, talking to the workers and thanking them for all their help. Then suddenly, I noticed that traffic ahead had slowed and stopped and people were staring off the road. As I continued up the road, I saw a minivan sitting down off the embankment with the air bag deployed. I immediately jumped out and ran down the bank to the van.

As I got closer to the vehicle, it became obvious to me that this was our friend Cindy Jo's car. I looked inside but couldn't see anything. I snatched the driver's-side door open and looked inside. To my surprise, a large body was laying across both seats, with most of it underneath the dashboard and glove box. I regained my composure and started to give immediate aid to the victim, our friend. I was beginning to get overwhelmed, thinking that I needed to react quickly to save Cindy Jo's life. I pulled her head and upper torso from under the dash and saw that her airway was obstructed with a large amount of blood. Her eyes were rolled back and she was unconscious. I start yelling at her, and then I got her all the way sitting up. I began to rub her face ever so gently to get her to recognize who I was and told her that she was going to be okay. She opened her eyes and asked me who I was.

I replied, "I am Sam, Cathy's husband."

She said, "I don't know you." She began to roll her eyes back again.

I screamed louder, "Cindy Jo, stay with me!" I was yelling and screaming for help when a local Columbus police officer arrived at the scene.

The police officer said, "Sir, do you think she is going to be okay?"

I grabbed my phone and hit speed dial for my stepson Jason Martin, a fireman who was on duty at his station in Columbus. I said, "Officer, tell him where we are and what we need. I need them to assist me in stabilizing her."

He took the phone, and Cindy Jo said that she couldn't breathe, and she began hyperventilating. I took my hand and placed it by her mouth and told her to breathe slowly. She acknowledged but was still in a lot of pain.

I yelled again for someone to open the passenger-side door so that we could have a free flow of air through the vehicle; some fresh air would help her breathe and maybe relax. As I got her stabilized, I continued to fight with her to keep her conscious till the EMS arrived. Once EMS arrived, I briefed them on the situation and her status, I told them that I had checked for any external obvious damage, and it appeared that the only injuries were to her face. I informed them that she was unconscious when I arrived, and I was able to get her up and she regained consciousness but tried to slip in and out. I helped them secure her neck with a neck brace as well as a back brace and help them carry her up the hill. I provided them with her purse so that they would have identification. Once EMS departed for the medical center, I went to the fire truck to get some sanitizing liquid to remove the blood from my hands and shoulders.

By this time, I had contacted Cathy, and she knew that I was fighting hard to handle this situation. I had seen this way too many times in Iraq, where I often came upon injured Soldiers and civilians and rendered aid, a constant reminder to me that life is so fragile. I tried to sleep Saturday night but I kept recalling the vision of seeing our friend in such a bad way; who wants to arrive on a scene and find a close friend in such bad shape? I laid awake most of the night and could only think that I needed to go to the hospital and see Cindy Jo.

Cathy and I woke early the next day, Sunday. We tried to relax and watch a movie; she fell back asleep in my arms, and the movie ended around 11 o'clock. She kept rubbing my hand in a similar motion like I had done for Cindy. She knew what I needed to do and asked me, "Do you want to go to the hospital and visit Cindy?"

I replied, "Yes, honey," so she got dressed and we proceeded to the medical center. We went to the information desk and the lady said visiting hours started at noon.

I said, "It looks like noon to me." We headed up to the eighth floor ICU and proceeded to Cindy Jo's room.

The head nurse stopped us as we entered her room to let us know she had just given Cindy some sleeping medicine; she was still in a lot of pain.

I asked ever so softly, "Can we just go in the room please?"

She replied, "Okay."

I walked in the room as Cathy stayed by the nurse; I immediately began rubbing Cindy Jo's right hand. Then I was amazed to what happened next. Cindy Jo began to say, "That feels so good. That feels so good."

I spoke softly so as not to startle her and said, "Cindy, do you know who I am?"

She begin to cry and said, "Sam, I love you. You saved my life. I remember you yelling, 'Cindy Jo, stay with me, stay with me.'"

She said, "Sam, you're my angel, God sent you to Cathy and now to me. I could see the light; I was headed home. You didn't let me go, you saved my life." She repeated that over and over again.

Cathy walked into the room and I said, "Cindy, Cathy is here too."

She started crying more, telling Cathy how lucky they both were and that I was an angel for them. She said she owed me her love, and over and over again, she said, "I love you, Sam."

The emotional stress on me at that point was overwhelming. I continued to remain calm and quiet. I gave Cindy a soft kiss on the forehead and quietly told her I loved her and I would be back after she rested. As we walked down the hall to the elevator, Cathy recognized that it was overwhelming to me again. When we arrived at the elevator, she gave me a hug and told me she loved me. We didn't say much as we walked to the truck; I opened her door, and then I got in.

We began to drive and Cathy asked, in a soft crying voice, "Are you okay?"

I thought for a second and replied, "Is God punishing me? Surely he knows what seeing this over and over again does."

She replied, "Everything happens for a reason. God let you survive the war because he had more for you to do. Today he wanted you to save Cindy Jo."

I hadn't thought of it like that. I spent the rest of the day with friends and family, trying to relax and enjoy the day. Sometimes I would find myself thinking about Cindy Jo, wondering if she was okay. Often I would remember similar events in Iraq, and then I drifted off to myself. Cathy would come and find me and pull me back in.

I have wrestled so much with the deaths of friends, fellow warriors, and even strangers. Is it my purpose to help others through difficult times, as God has helped me? I believe it is. I have pledged my life for months to help others; this weekend reinforced that pledge.

# CHAPTER 9

## Breaking the Silence of PTSD Struggles

Since I served in the Middle East for approximately thirty months, the thoughts and reminders of my time there come and go so often that I really cannot acknowledge them. It is also tough acknowledging them to peers or superiors without concerns that they may see weakness.

I had the toughest time dealing with these constant thoughts and reminders as I transitioned from a unit that frequently deployed to taking over duties as a Brigade Command Sergeant Major of a Basic Combat Training Unit at Fort Benning, Georgia. I continued to embody those traits and characteristics that I thought had kept me and my Soldiers alive for thirty-two months in the Middle East and incorporated them into my everyday work habits. The 192nd Infantry Brigade could not be doing better.

Unfortunately, for the first nine months, no one realized that their Brigade CSM was not doing well at all. I was able to perform my military duties on a daily basis without any negative thoughts whatsoever, until I attended a Soldier's Memorial Service in February 2006.

As I walked into the Chapel, my body began to tremble, and my mind began flashing back to memories of the sixteen Soldiers I had lost during my last deployment with Second Squadron, Eleventh Armored Cavalry Regiment (ACR). The Chaplain began to speak and then the roll call was given. My eyes began to water, and then tears rolled down my face like a waterfall. How did I get here? What was the root cause of all the issues? What did I see that triggered these constant memories? I had no control; being a warrior and a member of a team reduced to this was tough to swallow. After the roll call finished and we all stood up, I said, "Okay, the worst is over." Then, like a knife in my heart, the bugler began playing "Taps." My knees buckled and I couldn't feel my legs so I grabbed onto the front bench. The Brigade Commander, Colonel Charles W. Durr, Jr., looked at me and immediately knew this was having a negative effect on me. We talked briefly later that day about it being worse for me than any memorial I attended in Iraq.

After the memorial service, I began to lose control of my eating habits, and nightmares came every night. I began to work longer hours in order to not have any free time. The only problem is that you can only work so much! What triggered this? Are my fellow Soldiers having the same problems?

On May 5, 2006, while attending a course at Fort Jackson, it all came full circle when I found myself crying continuously for about an hour, thinking about those Soldiers who died in Iraq. I woke early in the morning from one of the worst dreams I ever had. It wasn't really a dream—I was there. I have seen the aftereffects of losing two great Company Commanders and seeing their bodies placed in bags. It was then that I began receiving counseling. I had been diagnosed in March 2006 with Post Traumatic Stress Disorder (PTSD), but like many leaders I put it off: too busy. Too busy almost cost me forever! From talking with Yvonne Wilbanks, Fort Benning's Alcohol and Drug Control Officer, I learned that PTSD must be treated early to avoid other serious problems such as depression and substance abuse. Her office, the Army Substance Abuse Program, had sponsored training on PTSD in conjunction with National Depression Screening Day at my unit.

While I did not develop substance abuse issues, I gained weight and was up to 260 pounds. Even at this weight, I was still able to run and do PT without problems from my weight. I thank God for the ACUs that covered that up. The weight issue has since been fixed through continued dedication and with the help of the medical staff at Troop Medical Clinic 5.

Later that summer, I was not feeling very well, so the primary physician's assistant sent me to the hospital to have some lab work done. Early the next morning, I received a phone call from the TMC; the caller sounded a little anxious.

She said, "CSM, you need to come to the TMC right now."

I replied, "I am in a meeting."

She said, "CSM, don't make me come get you."

I went into the physician's assistant's office, and he began to tell me about the lab work and how I was showing signs of heart disease. He said if I didn't do something about it soon, he couldn't predict the timeline.

We talked about the findings and about my family history; my father and his brother both passed away at the ages of sixty-four and sixty-five from heart disease, so my family history was a problem.

When I received this information, I had a booming blood pressure. I took a hard look in the mirror and continued receiving counseling from a combat stress doctor at Walter Reed Medical Center via the telephone. I also had been counseled by him during my last deployment in Iraq. I started dieting and working out harder and harder. The TMC folks continued to stay on top of me every day about my blood pressure checks and monthly lab work.

I found out during this period that the root causes of all my issues were the anxiety and the emotional instability I was dealing with from my extended stay in the Middle East.

Though we as leaders choose to fight most of our individual battles by ourselves, it's great to know we have excellent medical personnel who care about Soldiers of all ranks. We definitely don't appreciate them enough! Ms. Wilbanks had also told me leaders can be helpful to their Soldiers by being aware of symptoms of PTSD and making it a priority to get training and assistance for each Soldier. I believe my experiences have made me more sensitive to helping my Soldiers.

After six months, I lost more than forty pounds and could run like the wind again; I felt terrific! Emotionally, I still have issues whenever someone mentions a Soldier's death, but all in all, I have recovered to a degree.

Who would have thought a Soldier could have a PTSD incident while running down the road in a Garrison environment? I was running down Moye Road at about 0545 hours when, all of a sudden, three loud bursts of gunfire rang out. My heart felt like it stopped on the first burst. Then there was a second burst and then the third. My eyes began to water; I knew instantly what those three volleys were for. It was a firing squad from the First Battalion, 50th Infantry rehearsing for a funeral support mission. I tried to continue running, but I found myself remembering that time and time again, this has happened over the last four years.

Post-traumatic stress disorder, in my opinion, is not curable and will remain a part of my life forever. I am dealing with it by trying to replace any bad memories with the great memories of those fallen comrades and what this life is because of their efforts.

We as leaders do not get trained on how to react to losing our Soldiers or even losing our fellow leaders during combat. We continue to learn and grow through the struggles of our current conflict. It's an instinct to be a warrior. It's also an instinct to be saddened by the memories that come and go because of the loss of these great Americans. I am not able to develop the instinct to allow the memories of these events to disappear from my mind. Ms. Wilbanks explained that when these memories interfere with normal functioning, or if the thoughts turn to suicide, I need to get help immediately.

As I sat in the Forty-seventh Infantry Regiment's reunion last year, I talked to some of the heroes who fought in previous wars.

I talked to them specifically about what I was feeling and going through on a daily basis.

The best words I heard were, "Never forget, but let it go." I would add, "Never forget, get help, and let it go."

# CHAPTER 10

## Stigma

What is stigma? It's the phenomenon whereby an individual with an attribute that is deeply discredited by his or her society is rejected as a result of the attribute. Big words from a dictionary, but what does it really mean? I would challenge all of you that stigma is nothing more than fear of the unknown as it relates to post-traumatic stress disorder. Fears. We're soldiers; how can we be afraid of anything? Yes, we have anxiety about stuff, but we're not afraid, are we? I would say, as a leader, we have to demonstrate leadership; leadership is the ability to influence Soldiers to affect human behavior so as to accomplish a mission. Some leaders are apparently afraid of the unknown. While deployed to Iraq for over thirty-two months, I found myself riding down ͏ ͏ ͏pa, through Baghdad, Sadr City, and even Najaf with ͏ ͏ ͏hts: Where is the next IED? What will I do when it ͏ ͏ ͏es? Where is the sniper, and can he see us? Those are the thoughts that I had.

Now, as I sit here looking from a different perspective and experience a different kind of fear, I can't help but wondering what our leadership is afraid of. I know the answer; I have experienced it myself so many times over and over again. As we often do these days, I continue to attend funerals of Soldiers who have either lost their life in combat or killed themselves because of combat-related incidents. But didn't we all lose something? I truly think the answer is that we're afraid of losing again. Much like the Vietnam Era, when we came home and were spit on and called baby killers, now forty years later, we hear, "Thanks for your service." I heard that word often when I was in uniform or when I had a hat on that said something from the service. I looked at those people as they asked me questions, wondering, Are they really stupid or what? I am tired of hearing "Thanks for your service," "Thanks for what you do," and "Welcome home."

All of these words and a bag of Doritos won't begin to give back what was taken from most of us in combat. They keep trying, though; I came home from combat to a big sign and balloons that said "Welcome Home, Hero." A party followed, and we celebrated, hugged, and then life began again. But I wonder to myself often, as I watch our society, did I get a welcome home or was it a memorial service of a different kind? What! A welcome home memorial; yes, that's what I think happened to a lot of us. For those of us who didn't get a Purple Heart with visual wounds, we received a welcome home sign and a bunch of hugs, and then we moved on, or did we? I tried and tried over the past three years, almost to the date, to move forward with my life. I even managed to hide it from society for many months. Then I couldn't. Last spring I wrote an article that came out in *Infantry* magazine, called "Post Traumatic Stress Disorder Impacts All Levels of Leadership."

What the article didn't say was that the leadership of our country has been ordered not to place a stigma on any Soldiers who return with PTSD. We have even gone so far as to tell them you cannot use their combat experiences to disqualify them for a clearance. Wow, we have come a long way, haven't we?

The Chief of Staff of the Army issued guidance stating that it would put a full-court press on helping Soldiers with PTSD. What did that mean: observe, report, and discuss? That simply isn't enough to help us Veterans, current, past, and future. How are we handling the pressure of PTSD in our community? As I watch TV more and more to give structure to my postwar life, as well as prepare for retirement, I see more and more those words: "Post Traumatic Stress Disorder." These words are used a lot; it has become similar to a sports event, where we recognize a champion after winning a football championship, and then what? That is the end state that I want to get after with this article, now what? A typical Soldier serves his country proudly for multiple tours in Iraq and Afghanistan.

I find myself amazed at these orders when I know what the insiders are really doing. I spent a couple of weeks last summer and traveled to Hawaii; I talked to some World War II Vets, Vietnam Veterans, and those Soldiers we call heroes. To a man, they all said the same thing: "My supervisor asked me, 'What is your appointment for? What's wrong with you, you !@#$?!, you're faking, nothing is wrong with you.'" The Soldiers had no idea about what the Chief of Staff had said to his staff and the leadership of this country. As I looked at these Soldiers, I saw what I see in leaders' eyes every time they talk about PTSD: "Do I have this? Am I going to be singled out for having this disease?" I have seen many therapists since I came out to talk about how I am affected and what I feel is the best means of getting better. I put in my retirement request in April 2008 very reluctantly; I, too, was afraid—afraid of the future and what it had to offer me. I was directed by the Veterans Administration to go to another psychiatric brain surgeon in Columbus, Georgia, giving me the idea that apparently the doctors at Fort Benning were lacking something. The real story is that they wanted a third, fourth, and fifth opinion of sorts.

As I sat in the doctor's office and waited, I watched young kids who were getting treatment for child abuse and so on. Several Veterans had made this doctor their primary care physician and saw him on a regular basis. Finally, I got to see the doctor. He ·d. "Tell me about your combat experiences."

ement. "What do you want?" I

Iraqis, whom I had grown to love and appreciate to the degree I sponsored a family to come to the United States. I told him that I had mixed emotions after my first fifteen months of combat, so much that I figured out a way to return only one month after leaving the Middle East. Then dramatically, three months into that assignment, I was selected to be the Command Sergeant Major for an organization that would be deploying again, and I took that assignment as well. Several months into that tour, immediately following the death of two snipers, it started occurring. I told him the rest of the story up until that point. I started to talk to him about how I was trying to help others and how that helped me because it gave me a feeling of giving back. He shared with me details of senior officers had been visiting him since the war began to get private treatment. I was surprised at his words; was it really possible? The biggest fear is that it could be them.

Is PTSD contagious? I don't think so. It's not like HIV; you can't get it from a dirty needle. Is that what's wrong with our society? Are we afraid that if we shake the hand of a service member with PTSD we might get the same disease? Yes, I think it's possible that we are. I found myself feeling better that others have come to get treatment and he was helping them, regardless of who knew. That really is not the solution to resolving the fear of this disease. We have tackled this disease head-on; here is the Sam Rhodes cure for posttraumatic disease: You need to add structure, activity, support, and involvement in your life.

Yes, it's that simple: Place some structure in your life, get involved with the community and other activities, actively seek support and accept it at every turn, don't be ashamed for serving your country and defending this nation at its time of need, and finally, involve others that you trust and love in what's happening in your mind after it occurs. The psychiatrist's great extensions to assist the real professionals are those that you love and trust.

An example of involving my closest family to help me occurred on October 28, 2008. At 0615, as I prepared to head off to work, I was watching the morning news as I so often do. Then the news switched to a story out of Fort Bragg, North Carolina, where they were giving a young Soldier who lost both of his legs a new home. My eyes started to water; I immediately said good-bye to my wife—"See you after work, babe. Love you"—without letting her see my tears. I started the thirty-minute drive to Fort Benning. While I was driving, I started thinking about all the Soldiers whose memorial services I had attended. All the feelings of guilt that I had felt started to return: the instant memory of Captain Harding, who died without seeing his newborn child; the nineteen-year-old kid who never got to see his twentieth birthday; the son whose dad was killed just down the road from his Forward Operating Base; and that Warrant Officer who retired from the Army and came to Iraq as a civilian, who died in a IED attack, without a memorial service. The tears began to stream down my eyes. It became uncontrollable. I knew what I needed to do; I knew that it was too early to call my doctor. So I did one better, I called #1 on my speed dial. The phone rang and a wonderful voice answered: "Hi, babe."

I choked up and, with a tearful gesture, said, "I love you, babe."

Her wonderful voice began to console me: "What's wrong, babe? Why are you crying?"

I answered with what had happened; I explained to her my guilt, my anger of not having any wounds to show the world. The anger of not losing my legs for folks to acknowledge. I told her that I wished I had lost my legs; she said, "That would have been fine, babe; I would have loved you with no legs."

I was amazed, and tears of joy came down my eyes.

She said, "Babe, it's okay to cry; you're a wonderful, caring person; it's your nature."

I told her good-bye and finished my drive to work.

That's the answer to curing all of your worst nightmares. That's another story for another day. Just a note, though: There is nothing better than waking up to someone holding you after you just had the worst nightmare of your life! More blessing than you can imagine because of sharing and getting the ones you so dearly love involved in your healing. They want reduce the pain in your heart; they want to reduce the anxiety and stress that occurs. They will simply make you feel like you're not alone. Yes, the leadership of this great country has done a remarkable job of trying to reduce stigma about PTSD, but they need to do more. They need to tackle their own fear! Fear of the unknown. As I inch closer and closer to my last day in the military, I realize it more and more. When I came home, I was much like a warrior who gave his life, I was welcomed home with a big parade and a lot of hugs and handshakes, but then what? I will retire and become a Veteran and then …

We turn the next page without fear. Involve our past heroes and current heroes more and more in our day-to-day activities. Reach out to our Veterans and get them involved.

Let's tackle this disease without fear, together!

# CHAPTER 11

## Battle with PTSD and Suicidal Thoughts

I was never sure what the results of what I was doing would be, forgoing my life to do whatever the Army charged me to do, and now I find myself daily in unchartered waters. I know that one makes many mistakes in one's life; I have probably made more than my share. However, I have often tried to ensure that for every mistake I made, I placed more efforts to ensuring that they didn't reoccur. I have always tried to help others as a way of forgiving myself for the mistakes that I made.

Just less than two years ago, my life came full circle as the mistakes begin to mount, as my reflection of my combat experience and my continued guilt began to overwhelm me.

I chose an option that many have chosen without the opportunity to correct, and that was to take my own life. Fortunately, for some reason, I chose to give life a second chance and work harder every day to make up for my own failures, both as a man and as a father.

I have fought a battle every day since that day; depression, anxiety, and stress have made an impact in my life that few could bear. I bear that burden solely because of the folks in this picture.

My wonderful new wife and the daughter I love, who still doesn't recognize just what I would sacrifice for her happiness.

The Army's recent report of an increase in the suicide rate among Veterans sheds light on an important public health issue. It also highlights the need to create greater awareness around the challenges affecting the men and women serving in our Armed Forces, as well as the many services being offered by Department of Defense to address this problem.

One person who is committed to helping service members deal with the stressors associated with combat and deployment is retired Command Sergeant Major Samuel Marvin Rhodes, Sr.

After twenty-nine years of military service, CSM Rhodes retired January 1, 2009, and has begun a new chapter in his service to his country and comrades. In dealing with his own struggle with Post Traumatic Stress Disorder (PTSD) that led to suicidal gestures, CSM Rhodes has become an inspiration for members of the military nationwide, sharing his own experience with Veterans, Service Members, and families as well as visiting VA hospitals across the country and encouraging them to address and seek help for psychological health issues. CSM Rhodes's advocacy about the importance of seeking help among members of the military is not only saving lives, but helping to overcome the stigma associated with mental health issues.

Rhodes found inspiration in his father, Willie B. Rhodes, a WWII Veteran with a July 4 birthday. His father's experience in the military instilled a sense of service in Sam, a passion that has grown beyond the battlefield.

When Sam returned from the war, he found himself struggling with thoughts of suicide and would often replay scenes of explosions and gunfire in his mind.

"While attending a course at Fort Jackson, it all came full circle when I found myself crying continuously for about an hour, thinking about those Soldiers who died in Iraq," said Sam at a PTSD professional forum in 2007. "I had awakened early in the morning from one of the worst dreams I ever had. It wasn't really a dream—I was there."

After being diagnosed with PTSD while deployed in 2005, he decided to seek help, reminding himself how valuable his life is to those who love him. After getting treatment, Sam found a voice and inspiration within himself to share his story with other members of the military.

Over the course of the last year, I have struggled at times as the thoughts of suicide return more often than one wants to admit. The challenges of telling others how weak you feel are insurmountable. However, the passion for life and the understanding of it has caused me to survive it thus far. The battle will continue. I need only believe and build psychological resilience to prepare myself for those tough days.

In a moment in time, I found myself feeling guilty for my niece's husband Darrell losing his legs during a family vacation, after suffering an illness from eating oysters. I then was overwhelmed financially when I found out just how much it would cost to take care of a horse whose eye became infected while we were away. I asked myself over and over, would Darrel have gone on vacation had we not gone? If I was here, could I have caught the horse earlier to help it get better quicker? As I began asking myself those things, I found out my only son, who has been out of the Army for three years, has been recalled from the Inactive Ready Reserve. Though I support the Army at war, I have anxiety about sending my only son into combat. Just a day later, I learned that my former spouse had a heart attack and was air evacuated to the University of Alabama Medical Center for treatment. I am torn with concern for her well-being and the challenges that come each and every day.

I found myself on August 5, 2009, so overwhelmed with anxiety that it led to a depressive process that started to convince me that maybe it would be easier to say good-bye. As I thought about it more and more, I began to listen to my own words that I use when I speak across the country. I said, "You're a coward, what are you thinking? What about Jalen, Lianna, Kristopher, Tanner, and Jeffery? They will miss Papa." I thought Amanda, Sam, Kaitlynn, Kristi, and Jason; they will miss me as a father and stepfather as well. Most of all I thought about the huge sacrifice that Cathy has made to me. Yes, it's apparent that these thoughts never wander far, but it's good to have the start of the framework of psychological resilience to help when you need it most.

By talking to others and sharing my story, I have single-handedly improved my own desire to succeed and overcome these thoughts. I am known as a role model, but I'm just an everyday Soldier that struggles with the events that occur. Am I more receptive to harming myself as I battle through PTSD now, because of my deployments? Yes, but with the level of support available, it's an inspiration to help others help me.

"As a Soldier, I know most of the ways to get Soldiers to relax and talk," said Rhodes. "After [my first group] meeting, I have been encouraged to figure out a way to get more involved with helping Soldiers all across the country."

Rhodes is reaching out to Soldiers by sharing his story via the Mental Health Self-Assessment Program (MHSAP), a program of the nonprofit organization, Screening for Mental Health. The MHSAP offers Veterans, service members, and their families information on how to manage the stresses that often accompany deployment and provides self-assessments for a range of emotional issues. The assessments, which can be accessed at www. MilitaryMentalHealth.org or by calling 877-877-3647, are free and anonymous. After completing a self-assessment, individuals receive referral information including services available to them through the Department of Defense.

"Soldiers identify best with other Soldiers," said Rhodes. "We need more people like me to come out and share their stories, because those are the people who get through to members of the military who may need mental health help. We need to realize that I did all I could have done, but it wasn't enough at all. I have heard this every time someone talks about a Soldier who took their own life.

The Mental Health Self-Assessment Program is here to help connect Rhodes and others like him to fellow service members and Veterans that may be suffering silently. To find out how you can join this effort, visit the Mental Health Self-Assessment Web site at www.MentalHealthScreening.org/military.

# CHAPTER 12

## Second Generations of his family suffering with PTSD!

Willie B. Rhodes and his twin brother Earl Rhodes were born on Independence Day, July 4, 1920. They decided to join the war at a young age. Burl and Earl left to go to war by way of Camp Stewart. Burl decided to become a medic in the Army, not knowing what the future held, just wanting to defend his country and do his part. As it turns out, he may have done just that without a lot of effort.

During the Battle of New Guinea, Burl Rhodes was put to the test. A fellow Soldier, his Commander, Marvin Griffin, was seriously injured. Without hesitation, Rhodes made a decision that would impact his life forever. Griffin was bleeding from his wounds; Burl's natural instinct of caring kicked in; he maneuvered through fire, though seriously injured himself, to Griffin's side. He stabilized him enough to prepare him to move back toward a safe area for evacuation. Rhodes carried Marvin Griffin to safety, and he fully recovered. Rhodes did not know the impact of what he had done; he received numerous Presidential Citations for bravery and was awarded the Silver Star for his actions that day as well as many other military medals. Burl liked to talk about democracy and the home of the brave, but he rarely spoke of his own unique courage in World War II and his individual suffering from nightmares and symptoms of PTSD in the late seventies until his death on May 19, 1984.

Marvin Griffin later became Georgia's Lieutenant Governor and was seen as the successor to Governor Herman Tallmadge; Griffin won the governorship in 1954. Governor Marvin Griffin would not forget his friend. When the Governor was sworn in, Willie B. Rhodes was standing on the podium beside him. In 1955 and each following year, Marvin Griffin travelled to Burl's hometown to ride in the Independence Day parade with Burl Rhodes. A self-educated man, much like his fellow hero Alvin York, the Medal of Honor winner from Jamestown, Tennessee, Burl was proud to have served his country in its time of need. Like his son, he still had nightmares about his fiercest battles in war, but it didn't deter his love for his country and his fellow man. Willie B. Rhodes was a flag-waving American for sure.

Burl named his son Samuel Marvin Rhodes, after his fellow Veteran and the former Governor; Sam was born in Ringgold, Georgia in 1961. Little did Sam know he would be diagnosed with post-traumatic stress disorder (PTSD) after a lifetime in the military.

The young Rhodes had no idea what was in his future, nor did he even realize his destiny. At approximately six years old, the young Rhodes didn't understand why he was getting packages on occasion from someone he didn't know. By the time he was ten years old, Rhodes had had numerous conversations with the Governor's wife, as well as the Governor himself. He remembers them encouraging him to be a successful individual in life during each communication. Rhodes says his values were born of great mentorship from the Governor and his wife and his own parents. Governor Griffin offered to pay for the young Rhodes's college; however, he developed cancer soon after his first wife's death in 1978 and died in 1982 after a long battle with lung cancer.

Rhodes didn't lose faith; at the age of nineteen, he knew what he wanted to do. He enlisted in the Army as an infantryman and left his hometown. After twenty-nine years of military service, CSM Rhodes retired in January 2009. He spent three tours in Iraq and has begun a new chapter in his service to his country and comrades. In dealing with his own struggle with suicidal thoughts and symptoms of Post Traumatic Stress Disorder, CSM Rhodes has become an inspiration for members of the military nationwide, sharing his own experience with Veteran's and Active Duty Members and encouraging them to address and seek help for psychological health issues.

CSM Rhodes's advocacy about the importance of seeking help among members of the military is not only saving lives, but helping to overcome the stigma associated with mental health issues. CSM Rhodes mentions at every opportunity the effects of PTSD and the depression and anxiety that led to him having suicidal thoughts; he actually got a gun and would have killed himself had it not been for others recognizing he needed help.

Rhodes found inspiration in his father, Willie B. Rhodes, a WWII Veteran with a July 4 birthday. His father's experience in the military instilled a sense of service in Sam, a passion that has grown beyond the battlefield.

When Sam returned from the war, he found himself struggling with thoughts of suicide and would often replay scenes of explosions and gunfire in his mind. "While attending a course at Fort Jackson, it all came full circle when I found myself crying continuously for about an hour, thinking about those Soldiers who died in Iraq. I had awakened early in the morning from one of the worst dreams I ever had. It wasn't really a dream—I was there," Sam said. He was attending a PTSD professional forum in 2007.

After being diagnosed with PTSD while deployed in 2005, he decided to seek help, reminding himself how valuable his life was to those who loved him. After getting treatment, Sam found a voice and inspiration within himself to share his story with other members of the military. "Suicidal thoughts have remained a part of my thought process since 2007," he said. "I now continue to focus on the loss of my life and the impact of others. My message to them is don't cheat life and punish others.

"As a Soldier, I know most of the ways to get Soldiers to relax and talk," said Rhodes. "After [my first group] meeting, I have been encouraged to figure out a way to get more involved with helping Soldiers all across the country."

CSM Rhodes's free time is spent working with any organization that needs him to help our Veterans.

CSM Rhodes was awarded the Combat Infantry Badge, Bronze Star 1st Oak Leaf, Legion of Merit, seven meritorious service medals, and numerous other awards. He has attend every NCOES from PLDC to Sergeant Major Academy. He holds a master's degree in business administration and currently works as a project manager for Lockheed Martin, which is gracefully committed to his vision of helping his fellow warriors by allowing him to take these opportunities to share his story.

PFC Willie B. Rhodes was from a large family: three brothers, two sisters, six of his own children, and five stepchildren. Burl would always find time for his next of kin. Burl spent a large portion of his disabled vet time working with underprivileged children. He spent time teaching young people to care, about themselves and about others.

Like his father before him, CSM Rhodes also is a devoted husband and father; he is married to Cathy Rhodes, formerly of Lebanon, Ohio. They have six children and seven grandchildren.

# Chapter 13

## Reconnecting and Moving Forward

I owe most of you a heart-felt apology for not writing; it's amazing when you put all your eggs (or in this case, addresses) in one basket, it's hard to catch once the egg breaks and the yolk is gone. I searched and searched through all my stuff over the past several weeks and found your address.of Friends and Families who I felt have been apart of my life forever, but since I begin Battling with PTSD, I have felt anxiety as well as low self esteem. This has created a huge difference in my normal perspective and out look daily. I hope as part of the healing process that I begin sharing my struggles with all my relatives and friends who I served with over my Career. I hope all is going well. I hope to correspond a lot more so I will keep it simple and try to catch up.

On 6 April 2009 I visited the Arlington Cemetery; little did I realize how short life is. It broke my heart to see my fellow Soldier buried there. It also humbled me so much to relive their sacrifice over and over again.

In July 2005, while deployed on my third tour, I was diagnosed with PTSD; subsequently, I found ways until 2007 to manage through staying busy and medicine. In April 2007, it overwhelmed me and I considered and took all the appropriate action to commit suicide but by the grace of God, I didn't. Since that time, I have become a spokesman to help others on a daily basis; unfortunately, I got divorced during this process and now live in the Columbus, Georgia, area. Life has thrown me some curves but it wasn't without poor decision making on my own part. I chose to continuously go back to Iraq over and over for thirty months out of a thirty-two-month period.

I developed different thoughts and ideas about life that didn't correspond with other folks, and it left me on an island alone. Now through prayer and support, I have turn the page and now focus on other things; I recently completed my master's degree in business and now continue to serve my country as a retiree through public speaking.

Sometimes certainly we ask God's help and he puts us to the test to see how much we can handle; I was put to that test and somehow he has other goals for me that only he understands.

I continue to battle with PTSD, and suicide is never far from my mind. If I have a stressful time, my anxiety gets high and my thoughts of suicide return. Sometimes on the anniversary of my Soldiers who died in Iraq, I often relive those experience at night and consider other options. I have a great support group and I have pledged to contact someone when that occurs.

The reason I gave you this update is because most of you have been a part of my life for years; I love and miss you greatly. I hope to reconnect with you and correspond through phone calls or emails.

It's certainly your choice.

I am doing very well and recently returned from guest-speaking at Fort Gordon.

Love you guys,
Sam Rhodes

Dear General Casey,

On September 24th, 2009 I had the distinct honor of meeting Command Sgt. Major Samuel Rhodes. When I learned that a Soldier of his rank was speaking about his own PTSD, I felt compelled to attend his speech. Having listened to Sam share his personal experience, he mentions you numerous times in his presentation and spoke so highly of your commitment, I felt obligated to try to contact you. I feel there is a new level of awareness as a result of his mission.

Typically, I become very agitated and uncomfortable when listening to speakers address the topic of PTSD because it is usually textbook b.s. However when Sam spoke, I was on the edge of my seat. He had my full attention and there was not one statement made that I disagreed with. He was a breath of fresh air!

I believe that everything happens for a reason. His commitment has given him the opportunity to make a difference but he had to experience the suffering of PTSD first to understand and for this, my heart aches for him but he was chosen for a reason.

As the mother of a combat Soldier, I thanked him from the bottom of my heart for his tremendous courage to come forward to change the culture of silence. Through his personal actions, the level of awareness will increase and other Soldiers who valiantly struggle with this wound of war will realize, it is OK to be human and there is hope and help available.

My son is 100% disabled from PTSD as a result of his deployment to Iraq. My brave, courageous, handsome son, has spent the past six years as a walking time bomb, devoid of hope or joy for life. I have attended many seminars on PTSD and suicide prevention however none have been as impressive or compelling as this. After six years of struggling, I feel elated that change is coming and if we can spare one Soldier the pain of suffering, it is well worth the effort.

It takes tremendous courage for a military leader to step forward and acknowledge that he himself needs some help. This message is most significant to young heroes who feel ashamed for needing that help. They now have a leader to identify with and relate to. Just as any war machine needs maintenance, our Soldiers need mental and emotional maintenance during and after deployment. It is essential to treat PTSD as a wound of war and not a personal weakness.

It is only through awareness that the stigma of PTSD can be eliminated. Our leaders must continue to strive to challenge the culture of silence that exits within military and veteran life and raise the level of awareness to encourage support and counseling. We have a tremendous vet population and there is such a need for your words of wisdom and healing.

Sam's presentation is powerful and inspirational. I hope to have him return to visit us in Central MA and in particular to speak at the local Vet Center where he can reach many military members and veterans of all ages as well as their families. Family and friends are an integral part of any soldier's life. Services to inform and counsel those affected by PTSD are essential. We need to involve families in the healing process.

Your support of this mission is greatly appreciated and most necessary if we are to succeed. Our Soldiers are depending on us, they need to know we care.

Respectfully,

Rosemarie Annese
Vice President & Blue to Gold Liaison
Blue Star Mothers, MA Chapter 1

# Final Thoughts!

Today is January 9, 2010; it's been just over a year since I retired from the United States Army, since retiring I have traveled to approximately 52 events across out great country talking to Soldiers, Leaders and their Staff. It's amazing the stories that I get after each presentation that I conduct:

## Email # 1

Good Afternoon CSM Rhodes:

I had the pleasure of being in attendance last
Thursday the 10th for your briefing on PTSD and suicide
awareness. To begin I was emotionally touched for
use a better word by the passion of your work in
regards to Soldiers who suffer in silence. And some
who end there life because is empty and nightmarish.
I to suffer from PTSD. My tour was not as long as
yours and I'm not in any way shape or form going to
try. I served in B-Btry 1/103d Field Artillery "Hotel
Company" 89TH Military Police Brigade 2004-2005 and
where tasked with everything MP under the sun from IP
police Stations near Sadr City to PTSD Missions for
the Iraq Intern Government folks in the green zone.
I must have moved a few times From FOB Falcon, Fob
Blackhawk, FOB Trojan horse and got my bell rung a
few times VBIEDS, IEDs, Rockets and on and on .. But
enough stuff about me. The most Frighten thing is my
Son who is a medic with 702 BCB 2nd ID is heading out
there as I touched on to you, right after your talk.
And ya know what CSM I felt nervous in Baghdad, but
not being able to Cover my sons back is terrifying
to me. And has really fired me up, it like I just got

87

back, The sleep thing or lack of, patience is short.
My wife has said to me as a remember and I quote: I'm
not one of your F!@#$ Soldiers. So now I get to taste
the "Family father emotional side of this sacrifices."
that my Wife and Children felt when I was overseas.
That most will never know or want to feel. I would
appreciate any guidance you could give...

Always Forward Hooooooooah
**Name with Held!**


# Email # 2


CSM,

I went to your presentation on 10 September 2009, and
was very intrigue with what you had to say regarding
your experiences with dealing with PTSD. I'm writing
you to tell you my story from my experiences and
what I'm still going through and what I can do to
deal with my PTSD. In joined the Army Reserves in 20
August 2003. I went to basic and AIT,then arrived at
my unit. After 8 months of being in the reserves I
transferred to the RI National Guard. In September of
2004 I was assigned to a unit rifleman. In December we
were mobilized to Ft Stewart, GA. I deployed to OIF
III from May 2005 to May 2006. This is where the fun
begins.

The first 6 months in country we did combat
operations out of Camp Taji, patrolling in Hussnia
and Sadar City. I got hit by road side bombs and got
in numerous fire fights with the enemy as you know from
your experiences. Half way through my tour my unit was
moved to the An Albar Province doing convoy security
from Camp Al Asad to the Jordan border.

Around Christmas of 2005 my good friend was in a
hummv roll over during a night movement, which he
survived. On 1 January 2006, being the FSE for the
return convoy from Jordan, my hummv was struck, head
on by a civilian suburban going 80 to 90 mph. When I
was struck I was in the turret and the vehicle flipped

end over end. When I came to, I was being asked my SSN and that my medivac was inbound.

After I got medivac to balad, I then went to Qatar for 2 weeks. Then I returned to Iraq to see my doc and he said that I was good to return to duty, but I could barely walk. I returned to my unit then 2 months later I got sent back to Ft Stewart. Getting back to RI, I found out that my fiancé at the time was cheating on me and took most of my deployment money. On top of that I had nowhere to live. My unit returned from deployment. My friend I told you about earlier, was struck and killed in his truck by a drunk driver. That fueled my PTSD more and I got worse. I started to drink a lot.

I have been home from deployment for 4 years and have seen counselors but no result. My anxiety and depression are getting really bad. I'm married now and I'm taking a lot of my problems out on my wife. When I'm at work or around my buddies I deployed with I have no worries, but when I'm at home I just get angry, lazy or frustrated real easy. I can't sleep well and I have nightmares. I don't care about my money situation anymore. I always want to be alone or busy doing something to get my mind off of it. I'm always thinking about how I can go back to combat. I feel that I'm at peace with my mind when I'm there or I'm talking about it.

I don't think talking to doctors that have no experience with what I have been through is going to do anything for me. I definitely not going to kill myself because that is the easy way out and like you said today, "that would cause more problems for the people around me, than good." I guess I'm looking for advice from someone who has experienced it and is willing to listen. What can I do?

Your story and speech inspired me to reach out for help. I'm hoping that writing you this email will get me on the right track to getting help. Thank for your inspiration. In closing CSM, always remember "NEVER LEAVE A FALLEN COMMRADE."

### Name with Held!

# Email # 3

CSM Rhodes

I think the meeting the other day sort of touched home
with a lot of people but they wouldn't stand up and
ask questions.  I know as for me, I have pictures of
events that happen around me while I was deployed.  I
open up the computer at least once a week and look
through the pictures.  My wife will come and sit down
next to me and start asking questions and at first I
sort of kept everything inside but now I will talk
about almost everything that happened.  There are some
things that she won't understand.  I think in some way
at one time I was suffering but it wasn't war related.
In 1996 my first kid was born and I couldn't be home
for the birth because of deployment to Bosnia.  Also
in 1996 my grandfather passed away and I couldn't be
home because he wasn't immediately family and I was
deployed to Bosnia.  Finally in 1996, I was coming
home on R&R leave which turned to emergency leave
because my father was getting surgery and I was
requested to
be there.  We found out that he had pancreatic cancer
and they only gave him, at the most, 9 months to
live, this was in June.  I returned to Bosnia and in
August I received another Red Cross message that was
informing that he was sick and wasn't going to make it
through the night.  I came home after a few delays,
to make it for the first viewing and the funeral.
After I came home from Bosnia in September of 1996
my drinking increased and as the years passed it got
worse.  Finally in May 2004 I finally realized that my
biggest problem was I wouldn't talk about anything
that was bothering me. I woke up one morning after a
heavy night of drinking to realize I didn't
know what I had done the night before.  I started
talking about my problems to people I respected and
trusted and I have not had a drop to drink since.
If you want to use my small problem in one of your
talks that is fine with me.  I know my problem is
small compared to most but that was a tough year for
me.  Like you said everyone is affected by problems
differently. **Name with Held!**

It all started with Cathy and I was invited to San Antonio in January 2009 as a guest of the Army to speak at the Suicide Prevention Conference. I had never attended such event during my twenty-nine year Army Career. It was to say the least and eye opening experience that would fuel my Vision and commitment to change the Military's Culture of Silence about our battle with Mental Health Issues. Far too long we as Veterans and Warriors sit and wait while our minds dictate our own future. We sit still virtually while a time bomb ticks away until we make the critical decision. I ask myself while I sit on that plane how did I get here? What can I say to make a difference? I knew that answer already for I made such a decision in 2007, I was fighting the battle of a lifetime with Post Traumatic Stress Disorder, when I was Challenged by the Thoughts of Suicide that lead to me taking possession of a gun with bullets from a close friend. Whom I deceived by telling him I needed protection from a long trip which I felt uncomfortable about. He agreed and gave me the gun and even a class on how to use it.

As I reach this point I felt unresponsive to the challenges of life, the guilt from having survived the War, when other Greater men than I never returned. I fought through that daily until I reached out for help. I finally game forward after much encouragement from the Army's Substance Abuse Program Director that I could up others by sharing my own story. I was scared at first not sure how others would see me, a Senior Leader challenged by the one enemy you couldn't see coming until it hit you right in the face.

That enemy took me down but like most life challenging events you either get busy living or get busy dieing. I choose to live.

I find myself now even after all the presentations to others and even hearing their stories that make me thing, Damn, I really don't have it bad at all.

One Soldier approached me after presentation and said " CSM, I thought I seen everything, I was hit by a Vehicle Born IED, it killed my best friend and left with Traumatic Brain injury and part of my ear blown, they sent me to this Wounded Warrior Facility to recover. I was speechless, Listening eagerly to not show how humble I was by his words. He told me that just yesterday he was called downstairs by the Charge of Quarters, " Your wife is here", He told me his heart begin to race, he was so excited, it had been ten months since he saw her. I begin to smile, Then I was shocked by what he said next. I opened the door of the building and went outside, she was facing the road, I said her name and she turn to me with tears in her eyes, I could see why he said. I had been gone for 10 months and she was 4 months pregnant. It was a time bomb, I felt sick he said, I am off defending my country and she is back hear with someone else. The woman that I love so much did this to me. He told me you know, I thought the VBIED was the worse thing that could happen to me, "I was wrong".

I remained speechless for a moment as I gathered myself, I said his name, You know I really don't know what I would do if that was me, I would ask you to do one thing as you decide what to do. Think about her, She was back her every day not knowing whether or not you where going to return a life or not. That in itself is a daily Traumatic event that we take for granted to many times. Spouses seat at home waiting for their Husband's or Wife's to Return Wondering. Are they okay, do they need anything, Did they die to day.

The old saying goes, if they didn't come to my home by 2200 hours I can rest another night that they are okay. I couldn't even imagine it, A friend of my lost his son, I have had many Soldiers die in units that I served. I didn't die. I didn't know what it felt like to loose a son till my best friend lost his. I could only guess what your wife has been through, However to her credit she knocked on your hearts door today, to Say I am begging for your forgiveness. She wants an opportunity to come back to you, its obvious she loves you. It takes a hell of woman to admit a mistake. Sometimes we can see mistakes and know where their coming from. But in life mistakes happen that are not visible to negative eye. We can't correct them because others seemingly have forgotten how to forgive and forget. I concluded my thoughts with, she has a baby now. If you raise no matter whom the father might have been it's yours, she loves you and the baby needs a father. It's going to be tough but you can do it. Time and time again I shared similar stories to Young Men and Women, to each they all say the same thing. I never thought about it like that.

I find even some of our most senior Leaders are loving, caring and genuinely concerned about others. With a small catch to it, they lack initiative, they lack the credentials or the knowledge what to do next. All of them have no problem with the recognition, I have identified that this Soldier has a problem; I work with him every day. He leaves at 1700 hours and the next day he looks tired and like he is exhausted. He is always Angry as well. One such Great Leader approached me at the Pre-Command Course and humbled him-self to that end. It's nothing more than asking the right questions and showing that you care. He told me the story about a Soldier who worked for him who was also an officer who he knew personally that he had some issues. He said how I get him to recognize that and get help. I thought about it ever so briefly, and then I said. I think you already have Sir; it starts with recognition that comes from being a Great Leader and Caring. Our Soldiers can feel that you care, they can since that. We trained our Warriors to build the instincts to survive and win on the modern battle field. They now use that in their day to day life's. They know who cares and who is just going through the motions to their own end. I told him that I would approach it similar to many other opportunities that I had with Soldiers. Talk to our Chaplains, they are the first line of defense in the own going battle with the Mental Health related issues that are coming out after we return from War. Then ask the Soldier to go to lunch or even dinner to an area where all three of you could seat and eat and enjoy your time. TIME, Yes time is the key, the most valuable asset that you have that you share that you can never get back. Once you get the Soldier into this type environment, then you and the Chaplain or even another friend start talking about your own challenges of the War. Try to find a link between your own experiences and the Soldiers. This will close the Gap, when

I talk about my problems to others I find solute in the fact that they have been there, they have done that. When I talk to Mental Health Licensed folks, I don't feel that, time and time again I seat in a waiting room and listen. The Soldiers talk, I can't wait to get out of here "He don't Care" "How much are they paying him to listen". I have been there too. The Senior Leader looked at me and agreed, it was ironic that just hour after that I seat in a class with his spouse she brought up the same story. I felt that, if anything I cold leave there knowing that family was going to make a difference where ever they served, because they CARED enough to ask the tough questions.

I could go on and on for the over 1200 hours of presentations over the last year, it seems very small considering there are 8736 hours in a year, I didn't do enough. I only gave 1/8 of my time to helping others, I need to do more. Every Warrior has a story; Every Warrior wants to get help. The final story I will share is the one that has touched me the most.

I traveled in September to Rhode Island to speak to the Rhode Island National Guard and then travel to Boston to speak to the Boston Veterans administration. It was single handily the most eye open experience I have ever been apart of in my life. Time and time again, I say, "I haven't had it tough at all, never was so clear than during this visit. I talked several times, but the one that meant the most was a group session with about 30 Veterans and VA Staff. I started the dialogue about myself, The Veterans surprised me, and One Loud Spoken Navy Veteran caught my ear from the start. HE had attended another event, I wondering why he came back. He always sought me out and talk to me directly about what his life's goals where. He failed to mention until the last meeting that he was a homeless Veteran living in the woods of Boston. He talked about seeing his friend's life less after taking their own life, he told and expressed his dream of helping his fellow Veterans. This man was one of the brightest I have ever dialogued with, He could find work, and he could make his way out of the area. His commitment to help others and remaining that environment was impressive to say the least.

I spent several more moments talking to this gentlemen, he ask me for my number. Reluctant as I am about giving out my number I throw it at him hoping that he would call. To my surprise he did, he called time me time again. Each time updating me on what he was doing and what he had going own. The hard part about it he was using his last dime to call me from a phone booth. Was I worth that much, he continued to think me for coming, couldn't wait to see me again. I was again without words.

As you can see the year as been long, I ended the year with a strange ending; it always seems to come by way. I received a call from my Lockheed Martin Program Manager on the day by Nephew died, yes, that's another story for a different day. He told me his Boss and he wanted to have a conference call with me on the following day, the anxiety begins. I was wondering time and time what is happening. I didn't know. Finally I convenience him, that I needed to have an idea what the topic was. He informed me that I had won **2009 Community Service Award Build Effective Relationships**. I was surprised, Speechless again. I was told that the following week they would travel to Fort Benning to provide me with a plaque, etc.... I told Cathy and several of my closes friends attended. To each person they all said the same thing, Sam, Finally your getting the Recognition you deserve. As the award ceremony concluded, I was given the opportunity to speak. I am never usually a loss for words. As I begin to speak I was loss for words, my eyes water ever so slightly. I reached down and begin to speak, I said I greatly appreciate this award, you know just this past week Darryl died and I found myself wondering was the time and effort that I was given to help others worth it. This award reemphasis that I am on the right path, it is worth it. I asked each of them to do one thing this New Year if nothing else, to reach out to one Veteran and give them a hand. I know once that happens, they want never stop.

This book is dedicated to the once that Sacrificed it all and gave their life, It's also in hope that the future is brighter for those that gave all still fight the e enemy within.

I would leave you with this thought; have you walk the walk, until you have felt the pain, until you have consider the choice between living and dieing from your own hands. Think about the choices they where faced. Like many of my fellow Veterans and Warriors we have. I find myself writing that final letter time and time again in my own mine after the challenges of a given event in my life or a memory of those I want to forget.

"Please Forgive me, I find myself challenge with life, I continue to feel quilt and Angry, I have failed miserably, Do not blame your self for my Actions, etc ..." I Pray that like my Vision to help, I prevent others like me from never signing it.

GOD BLESS OUR Troops Past, Present and Future

Please HELP us HELP Ourselves!

After being apart of this Operation Iraqi Freedom since Apr 2003, I find myself as the resident expert about a lot of things. The day to day business as usual is different for me based on my current experience level compared to those around me. As the heat started rising in May 05 the Soldiers would stop and talk as normal and most of them would begin their conversation with "CSM it sure is hot". I would almost every time reply with. "Soldier, You better be drinking water it's not hot yet". They would leave and say "HOOAH" CSM. I knew having been in Iraq for the previous summers that the heat would come in August and then it would turn cold in September. Like our country they have a consistent weather pattern.

Recently, in the last week I crossed path with a Warrant Officer in my area and it brought back memories of a fellow American Carl Carroll a retired Chief Warrant Officer 4, working for the TITAN company was killed after departing my FOB to go to BAGHDAD in 2005. This was and remains a tough thing for me to swallow in my book. Alot of Americans do not realize that we Service members cannot do our job without the support of the TITAN Companies and Halliburton's. They have given us a quality of life that most Soldiers only dream about. The quality of life is unprecedented in previous Wars. Still we have service members who do not realize that their fellow Veterans before us did not have these luxuries. I for one appreciate all Americans who have volunteered to come into harms way and support our troops.

**Post Traumatic Stress Disorder (PTSD), Suicide Prevention, Psychological Resilience And Comprehensive Fitness**

**CSM (Ret) Samuel Rhodes**

**"Changing The Culture of Silence"**

**samuel.marvin.rhodes@us.army.mil**

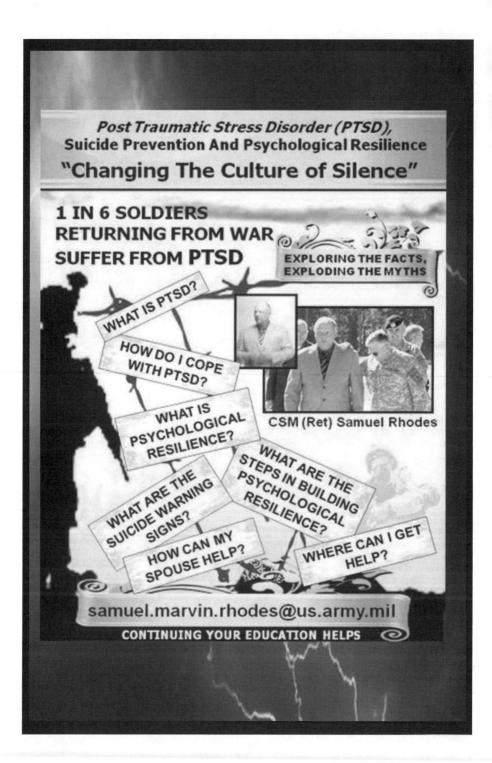

# What IS Post Traumatic Stress Disorder (PTSD)

## PTSD is a disorder that sometimes occurs after a traumatic event such as:
- Combat or military exposure/ Terrorist attacks

## PTSD symptoms can start immediately after the event or months and even years later.

# PTSD (Trauma) May Occur With Other Problems:

- A loss of feelings of safety
- Feeling broken or damaged
- Low energy
- Sexual dysfunction
- Anxiety
- Irritably, anger, and resentment
- Emotional numbness
- Withdrawal from normal routines and relationships

- Difficulty making decisions
- Unexplained chronic pain
- Sleep disturbance
- Depression
- Feeling out of control
- Restlessness
- Sense of fairness in the world lost
- Increased need to control everyday experiences

Excessive weight gain

Good Cholesterol was bad

Bad Cholesterol was Worse

Signs of Heart disease

High Blood Pressure

# The Statistics are Startling

According to a VA study of 168,528 Iraqi veterans, 20 percent were diagnosed with psychological disorders, including 1,641 with PTSD.

➢ An earlier VA study found that almost 12,500 of nearly 245,000 veterans visited VA counseling centers for readjustment problems and symptoms of PTSD.

➢ Enlisted Soldiers were twice as likely as officers to report PTSD.

➢ A Defense Department study of combat troops returning from Iraq found 1 in 6 Soldiers and Marines acknowledged symptoms of severe depression and PTSD, and 6 in 10 of these same veterans were unlikely to seek help out of fear their commanders and fellow troops would treat them differently.

➢ A study published in the New England Journal of Medicine said about 1 in 6 Soldiers returning from Iraq suffered from PTSD. Interviews with those at risk showed that only 23 percent to 40 percent sought professional help, most typically because they feared it would hurt their military careers.

# Soldier Suicides
# May Set Record

More U.S. military personnel took their own lives in 2009 than were killed in either the Afghanistan or Iraq wars last year, according to a Congressional Quarterly review of the latest statistics from the Armed Services.

## SUICIDE STATISTICS

• At least 334 members of the military services committed suicide in 2009, compared with 297 killed in Afghanistan and 144 who died in Iraq during the same time period.

• In 2009, the Army had 211 of the 334 suicides, while the Navy had 47, the Air Force had 34 and the Marine Corps (active duty only) had 42.

# Psychological Resilience

- Resilience in **psychology** is the positive capacity of people to **cope** with **stress** and **catastrophe**.

- It is also used to indicate a characteristic of resistance to future negative events. In this sense "resilience" corresponds to cumulative "protective factors" and is used in opposition to cumulative "risk factors".

- The phrase "risk and resilience" in this area of study is quite common. Commonly used terms, which are essentially synonymous within psychology, are "resilience", "psychological resilience", "emotional resilience", "hardiness", and "resourcefulness".

# Ten Steps to Build Resilience

**1. Make Connections**
Good relationships with close family members, friends or others are important.

**2. Avoid Seeing Crises as Insurmountable Problems**
You can't change the fact that highly stressful events happen, but you can change how you interpret and respond to these events.

**3. Accept That Change Is a Part of Living**
Certain goals may no longer be attainable as a result of adverse situations.

**4. Move Toward Your Goals**
Develop some realistic goals. Do something regularly — even if it seems like a small accomplishment — that enables you to move toward your goals.

**5. Take Decisive Actions**
Act on adverse situations as much as you can. Take decisive actions.

**6. Look for Opportunities for Self-Discovery**
People often learn something about themselves and may find that they have grown in some respect as a result of their struggle with loss for life.

**7. Nurture a Positive View of Yourself**
Developing confidence in your ability to solve problems & trusting your instincts helps build resilience.

**8. Keep Things in Perspective**
Even when facing very painful events, try to consider the stressful situation in a broader context and keep a long-term perspective. Avoid blowing the event out of proportion.

**9. Maintain a Hopeful Outlook**
An optimistic outlook enables you to expect good things will happen in your life. Try visualizing what you want, rather than worrying about what you fear.

**10. Take Care of Yourself**
Pay attention to your own needs & feelings. Engage in activities you enjoy & find relaxing.

# Comprehensive Soldier Fitness

COMPREHENSIVE SOLDIER FITNESS
STRONG MINDS ★ STRONG BODIES

**5 DIMENSIONS OF STRENGTH:**

- ➤ PHYSICAL
- ➤ EMOTIONAL
- ➤ SOCIAL
- ➤ FAMILY
- ➤ SPIRITIAL

U.S. ARMY

# Comprehensive Soldier Fitness

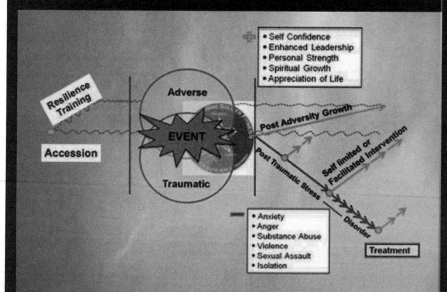

Bottom Line: A Soldier that has strong Comprehensive Fitness has decreased injury severity (mentally and physically) and recovery times.

# Effects on Our Soldiers & Families

**Positive**
**Motivated**
**Can do**
**Energetic**
**Situational Awareness**

**Tired**
**Depressed**
**Apprehensive**
**Distracted**

## What's in the Army's Rucksack

- Higher Divorce Rates
- Increased Suicide Rates
- Increased Alcohol and Substance Abuse
- Increased PTSD and Mental Health Issues
- Increased Domestic Abuse
- Higher Sexual Assault Rates
- Above average attrition of future leaders

# Global Assessment

1. Comprehensive Soldier Fitness Website

http://www.army.mil/csf/

2. Click on Resource Link

http://www.army.mil/csf/resources.html

3. Click on Soldier Fitness Tracker Link

https://www.sft.army.mil/

4. Click on CAC/AKO Login Link

5. Click on Continue to GAT link

6. Click on Begin Survey

**Soldier Fitness Tracker**

Please respond to the following items. Be honest – there are no right or wrong answers!

| | Not like me | Not much like me | Somewhat like me | Mostly like me | Very much like me |
|---|---|---|---|---|---|
| I have been obsessed with a certain idea or project for a short time but later lost interest. | ○ | ◉ | ○ | ○ | ○ |
| Setbacks don't discourage me. | ○ | ◉ | ○ | ○ | ○ |
| I finish whatever I begin. | ○ | ○ | ○ | ◉ | ○ |
| I often set a goal but later choose to pursue a different one. | ○ | ◉ | ○ | ○ | ○ |
| I can do just about anything I set my mind to. | ○ | ○ | ○ | ◉ | ○ |

How well do these statements describe you?

| | Not like me | Not much like me | Somewhat like me | Mostly like me | Very much like me |
|---|---|---|---|---|---|
| I am good at changing myself to adjust to changes in my life. | ○ | ○ | ○ | ◉ | ○ |
| I have a flexible attitude about life. | ○ | ○ | ○ | ◉ | ○ |
| It is difficult for me to adjust to changes. | ○ | ◉ | ○ | ○ | ○ |
| I can usually fit myself into any situation. | ○ | ○ | ○ | ◉ | ○ |

## -30 MIN COMPLETION

## CONFORMATION OF COMPLETION SENT TO COMMAND

We are currently developing a more comprehensive fitness program that elevates mental fitness to the same level as physical fitness. The effects of repeated tours is cumulative; they are wounds of war and nothing to be ashamed of.

CSA GEN George W. Casey, Nov 2009

# Where To Get Help

- National Center for Post Traumatic Stress Disorder
  (800) 296-6300 or http://www.ncptsd.va.gov

- Military One Source
  (800) 342-9647  (If overseas precede number with U.S.
access code)

- Military Mental Health Organization
  www.mentalhealthscreening.org

- National Depression Screening Day
  www.MilitaryMentalHealth.org (anonymous screening)

- Emergency call 911

- Chaplains, Troop Medical Clinics,
  Mental Health Providers, Emergency Room,
  and National Depression Screenings

Photos provided by:
Sam Rhodes

At the end of the day, no matter how much effort we spend on programs, how many changes we make to policies, or hours spent on suicide prevention training, our last and most potent line of defense remains our leadership.

VCSA GEN Chiarelli, JAN 2010

samuel.marvin.rhodes@us.army.mil

Questions?

# WOUNDED WARRIOR
# HORSEMANSHIP

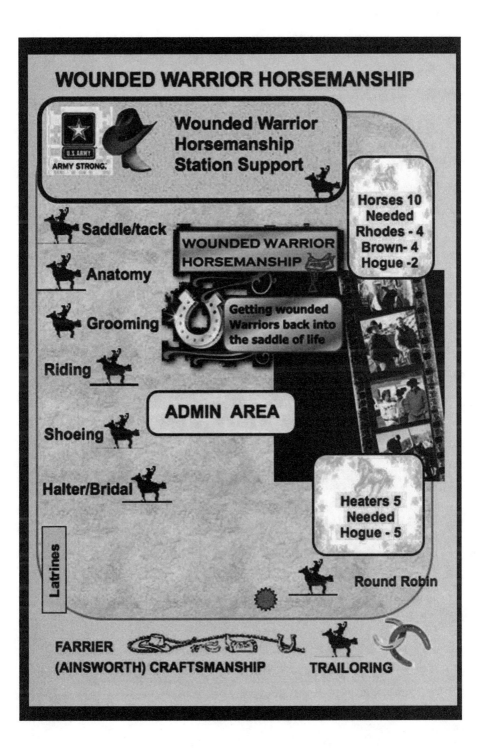

# Psychological & Physiological Benefits of Human-Equine Interaction & Horsemanship Training

- Pilot programs at Walter Reed Army Medical Center, Brook Army Medical Center, and Ft. Hood Physical Therapy Program have looked at the effects of equine-assisted therapies with wounded warriors from Iraq and Afghanistan.

- These programs have worked with seriously injured soldiers and amputees with improving the healing process through by incorporating horsemanship and riding into the therapeutic regiment.

- The pilot programs have shown improvements in the following areas: self-confidence, morale, sense of accomplishment, balance, coordination, and body awareness.

# Psychological & Physiological Benefits of Human-Equine Interaction & Horsemanship Training

- Soldiers who participated in the pilot programs stated that benefits were also derived from the "outside the box" nature of the training. Soldiers sited leaving the hospital setting, understanding they could accomplish what they tried, and promoting an idea of a future with possibilities as reasons for their improved outlooks on recovery.

- The Harris County Cattlemen's Association, in conjunction with the Harris County High School Rodeo Team sponsored a Wounded Warriors Horsemanship Program March 2009. This program included a rodeo demonstration by the Harris County Rodeo Team, education and training on various aspects of horsemanship, and horseback riding for Warriors in Transition.

# Psychological & Physiological Benefits of Human-Equine Interaction & Horsemanship Training

- The Wounded Warriors were given riding lessons in the arena. The Soldiers were able to apply the skills they had learned that morning through practical exercises. The Soldiers started riding with the high school students and volunteers.

- As they demonstrated the ability to led the horse on their own they were able take the reins and ride freely around the arena. All Soldiers were able to demonstrate the ability to get their horse to move, stop, and follow directional commands.

- In order to perform these tasks the WT had to incorporate the lessons learned in the previous training, and to demonstrate body awareness, coordination, balance, and self confidence. All the Soldiers responded that they felt a sense of accomplishment, self-confidence and improved morale.

# Psychological & Physiological Benefits of Human-Equine Interaction & Horsemanship Training

- **Lastly, all participants (Soldiers, Cadre, volunteers) had a fellowship dinner of steak, baked potato, salad, and beans, which was donated by the Cattlemen's Association.**

- **The Soldiers interacted with each other and the volunteers.**

- **They recalled stories about the day's experiences and expressed a strong desire to see this program repeated in the spring.**

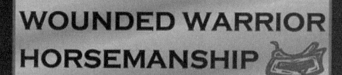

**WOUNDED WARRIOR HORSEMANSHIP**

**Getting wounded Warriors back into the saddle of life**

**Warriors ride to recovery**